JIMMIE DAVIS

AF270937

Girls' Ministry
IDEA BOOK

LifeWay Press®
Nashville, Tennessee

ISBN: 9781415867297
Item: 005190078

Dewey Decimal Classification: 259.23
Subject Heading:
GIRLS \ TEENAGE GIRLS \ CHURCH WORK WITH TEENAGERS

Printed in the United States of America.

Student Ministry Publishing
LifeWay Christian Resources
One LifeWay Plaza, MSN 144
Nashville, TN 37234-0144

We believe that the Bible has God for its author; salvation for its end;
and truth, without any mixture of error, for its matter and that all Scripture is
totally true and trustworthy. The 2000 statement of *The Baptist Faith and Message*
is our doctrinal guideline.

Table of Contents

About the Author

Jimmie Davis serves on the student ministry staff of First Baptist Church, Spartanburg, South Carolina, as the director of girls ministries. Jimmie is passionate about mentoring teen girls and trains women to lead girls' ministries in churches across America. She is the author of *Girls' Ministry Handbook* and has a deep desire to multiply ministry by training and equipping others. Her goal for ministry in the future is to pass the torch well and leave a legacy of loving God to younger women.

Jimmie served with her husband, Sam, in youth ministry for over 25 years. Sam is now the Associate Pastor at First Baptist Church, Spartanburg. Sam and Jimmie are very proud of their two adult children. Jordan and his wife, Stacy, and Ginger and her husband, Derek, are all involved in serving the Lord in ministry. They have three wonderful grandchildren—Kade and Kyle are identical 3-year-old twins and Kendall is a 5-year-old little princess. Jimmie's favorite pastimes are traveling, spending time with her family, and being the best MiMi she can be.

Dedication
In loving memory of my Mother, Annie Lou Leonard,
who looks down from heaven.
I know she is proud of what God is doing through me!

Special thanks:
To my Lord and Savior Jesus Christ
who has kept His hand on me throughout my life

To my family:
Sam, Ginger, Derek, Jordan, Stacy, Kendall, Kyle, Kade, and Daddy. You have
supported, loved, and encouraged me, which has given me the courage
to attempt something I never thought I could do!

Pam Gibbs and the LifeWay staff:
You have been wonderfully encouraging and helpful during this process.
I know you spent many hours editing and guiding me!

Introduction

Congratulations! You have started a girls' ministry in your church. But now that you are in the trenches, you may find ministry to teenage girls is more complicated than you thought. How do you design ministry that really makes a difference in the lives of teenage girls? Who are these girls anyway—the postmodern generation? And now the iGeneration? Exactly what does that mean and how do we design contemporary ministry that goes past the 70s, 80s, and 90s mind-sets? Maybe you are trying to model girls' ministry after your women's ministry, and it simply is not working. Or perhaps you are going from one event to the next without any real impact on their lives. Maybe you are at a roadblock and really don't know which way to turn.

The *Girls' Ministry Idea Book* will challenge your thinking and give you ideas that will enable you to get the attention of teen girls despite the complications that plague their generation. Through these ideas, you will be able to teach spiritual truths that will change their lives forever. Many of the concepts in this book are events and ideas that I have tried over the past five years as the director of girls' ministry in the church where I serve. Some have worked well and become traditions. Others didn't work as well for the personality of our group, but they may fit your group perfectly. You will need to take these ideas and modify them to meet the needs of the girls in your church. Each group of girls is unique because of the area in which they live, their family backgrounds, their spiritual maturity, and the personalities that make up the group.

I pray the *Girls' Ministry Idea Book* will give you the methods and ideas to reach girls with the love of Christ and transform their lives forever.

—Jimmie Davis

CHAPTER 1

Communication
with iGeneration Girls

*D*O YOU REMEMBER hopping on your bicycle, riding to your friend's house, and talking all afternoon on the front porch about all the things important to a teenage girl? If you do, I can almost guarantee that you grew up in the 60s, 70s, or 80s. For the most part, a teenage girl in today's culture has no concept of riding her bike to a friend's house or sitting on the porch. Instead, she communicates with her friends via text messaging, cell phone, Facebook®, and other forms of online social networking. They live in a technology-driven world. We can view technology as a threatening enemy, or we can utilize it as an effective tool to reach this generation of teenagers.

Relationships are indispensable in girls' ministry. You probably have heard the adage, "People really don't care how much you know until they know how much you care." That is true with this generation as much as it has been with any other. Being connected with others emotionally and socially has always been a deep need in the hearts of teenage girls (God created women as relational beings), but such connections are even more important with this generation. In past generations, girls waited to get letters from the stagecoach and waited anxiously to see their beau riding up on a horse to sit in the parlor. With the development of the telephone in 1876, communication became easier and more frequent.

With public transportation and the development of cars and airplanes, staying connected became commonplace. However, the world—and communication—changed forever with the development of personal computers and the Internet. The Web has made communication instant and constant. News, information, and communication are accessible at the click of a button, and girls can't seem to do without instant socialization and online networking. Yet, even though communication is constant, the connections girls need at deeper levels aren't happening. This is the most connected generation in some respects, but it is the most disconnected and distant generation in other respects. How does this change the way we communicate with teenagers? How do we as leaders keep connected with girls from the iGeneration (Internet Generation)? Often, we as adults lag behind in adapting to and using technology and must work hard to keep up with it. Technology is changing so rapidly in our modern world that by the time this book is printed, technology will have changed again, so many of the ideas I present will be simply that—ideas. You'll have to adapt these thoughts to changing technology and resources. I pray this book and the ideas presented here will cause you to think creatively about this generation, and I pray that you will stay so in tune with God and His Word that you will know how to communicate the gospel in a relevant way to the girls in your church and community.

Technology is changing so rapidly in our modern world that by the time this book is printed, technology will have changed again.

Not only is technology changing, but vocabulary is changing as well! Today's teens often do not understand words we use, and we completely misunderstand the words they use. Often teens use words that are not offensive, but they sound offensive because adults do not know what they mean. If you hear a word you don't understand, don't be embarrassed to ask. Asking and learning is an effective way to build relationships.

Sometimes this generation of girls use words that are crude, rude, and unacceptable to the older generation, but they mean something completely different to the girls. If a girl uses a word that is offensive to you, ask her what it means to her. Then explain what it means to your generation. This will help her understand how she is perceived, and she will be more careful of how she uses the word around others.

EFFECTIVE COMMUNICATION

The following ideas for communicating effectively to this generation of girls can be adapted to meet the needs of the girls in your church or community. If you are uncomfortable with technology or are a novice, don't allow those roadblocks to keep you from reaching girls. Ask the girls to help you. They love helping others and being "experts" in an area. And your asking for help enables them to see that you are unafraid to admit an area of weakness— a lesson they desperately need to learn themselves.

✿ **Facebook**®: If you want to get word out to the girls in your church, a great way to communicate is via Facebook. To get started, you will need to register at *www.facebook.com*, set up your profile, and then invite the girls to be your friend. The Web site is secure in that only approved friends can view Facebook profile pages. When you are successfully set up on Facebook (you may have to recruit the help of a teenage girl to get you started), you can send out invitations to events, Bible studies, and so forth, and girls can RSVP online by accepting, declining, or giving you a "maybe" response. Using Facebook is an awesome way to know how to plan and be prepared for the number of girls coming. Girls will be able to see who is coming, and when they know their friends will be there, they are more likely to come. You can also post pictures of events and communicate back and forth with the girls in your group on a regular, instant basis.

Facebook also allows you to see the girls' pages and know what is going on in their world. You can set up a special group for your girls' ministry and invite girls to join. There you can post information and allow girls to post information back as well.

Facebook also lists birthdays of your accepted friends, so it is easy to keep up with birthdays of girls in your group. Just post a quick message, send a Facebook gift, or even record a video birthday song. I received more birthday messages this year than ever before in my entire life. It was a special day for me to receive wishes from girls and from friends that I rarely talk to or see.

Keep in mind that comments made on another person's wall can be seen by their friends. Girls often forget this bit of information, and we need to be aware of it as well. Never post anything on Facebook that would betray a confidence such as, "I'm praying for the bad situation with your parents" or "I'm praying for you as you overcome your struggle with pornography." "I'm praying for you today" is sufficient. If something private does need to be discussed, you can send a message, as those are only viewable by the person to whom you send it.

One other note: be careful about the friends you accept. If you accept someone and she has inappropriate content on her Facebook page, you can delete her as a friend or even report the inappropriate content to Facebook.

✿ **Blogging devos:** Blogging is simply typing your thoughts and ideas in an online journal (or Web log; "blog" for short) of sorts so others can read them. You can blog your thoughts, things God is teaching you, and devotions for the girls in your ministry. The girls can post comments on your blog. It is a fantastic way of keeping in touch. Just remember that on some blogging sites, anyone can see what you are writing. If you blog on Facebook, then only your accepted friends can see what you write. A few blogging Web sites you might consider include: Blogger (*www.blogspot.com*); WordPress (*www. wordpress.com*); and LiVEJOURNAL (*www.livejournal.com*).

✿ **Text messaging** is a great way to stay in touch with the girls in your group and let them know you are praying for them or to get information to them. Most teenage girls have cell phones, and many can send and receive text messages. It is important to check with the girls to make sure they can send and receive messages with their cell phone plan. You don't want to cause undue costs.

While the girls were still hanging upside-down in their seat belts, one of them grabbed her cell phone and sent a text to her discipleship group asking for prayer!

At our church, text messaging had a big impact on a scary situation. In our girls' discipleship groups that meet every Sunday night, the girls become very close, pray for one another, and hold each other accountable. Recently, three girls were involved in a serious car accident. A young man on a motorcycle ran a traffic light, hit them broadside, and flipped the girls' car. While the girls were still hanging upside-down in their seat belts, one of them grabbed her cell phone and sent a text to her discipleship group asking for prayer! This was a frightening time for these girls, and texting was their avenue for instant prayer and support. Their discipleship leader was waiting at the emergency room when they arrived in the ambulance. Those girls will never forget that she was there in their time of need.

✿ **Twitter®** is a social networking and micro-blogging service that allows users to let others know what they are doing at that moment by posting their own status and reading other users' updates, known as "tweets." Updates are displayed on the user's profile page and delivered to other users who have signed up to receive them. The sender can restrict delivery to those in his or her circle of friends. Users can receive updates via the Twitter Web site, their cell-phones, or by e-mail. Twitter (*www.twitter.com*) is an easy, quick way to tell others exactly what you are doing at any time. You can also update your status on Facebook via Twitter.

✿ **Online social networking for your church:** Some churches set up social networking tools on their church's Web site. Students can sign up and network with other members of the youth group. You can communicate with students, and they can post their thoughts. Students like having sites to which only the students and youth leaders from their church have access. Of course, the idea is to include as many students as possible in order to reach them for Christ.

✿ **E-mail, land lines, voice mail, and snail mail:** I never thought I would see the day when e-mail or voice mail would be obsolete, but for the most part, the iGeneration thinks e-mail is old-fashioned, and most don't check their voice mail. It's too slow. Why would they want to e-mail or take time to check a voice mail when they can send a text anywhere, anytime? It's important to know the girls in your church and find out how they prefer to communicate. Sending a text message, Facebook message, or calling on their cell is definitely the way to go with most of today's teens. Nevertheless, with all of the instant technology available today, it is still special for a girl to receive a nice card or note of encouragement in the mail. I know girls who carry special cards in their Bible. One girl even framed a card she received from her youth minister.

AFFIRMATION SERVICE

Girls need to hear encouraging words from other people. From time to time, it is important to set aside a special time of affirmation for your girls to encourage each other in their faith, relationships, and daily walk. Communicating encouraging words is a part of developing close relationships with girls. In the girls' discipleship groups in our church, we set up a time at least once a year to affirm each other. There are several ways you can set up affirmation times for your girls depending on the size of your group. Here are some ideas for different group sizes:

✿ **Small group:** If you have a small group of four to six girls, it is easy to allow each girl to verbalize her affirmation for every girl. The atmosphere is important. You may want to set up the room so that the girls are sitting in a circle where they can all see each other, or you may want to set up the chairs in a semi-circle with the "affirmation chair" as the focal point.

If you are doing this in a home, you can direct the girls how to sit depending on the set-up of the furniture. Candles along with soft praise and worship music playing in the background provide an atmosphere in which girls' hearts are tender and not distracted.

Start the time by reading a short Scripture and praying. Talk about some important things that have happened in the group over the past year. You may want to talk about how you have seen the group grow and how you have seen God change their lives as a whole.

From time to time, it is important to set aside a special time of affirmation for your girls to encourage each other in their faith, relationships, and daily walk.

Briefly give the ground rules for each girl speaking. You may want to say, "Tonight is a time where we will affirm one another in how we have seen God work in each other's lives. Affirming means you will say positive things to build up each other. Pray that God will impress on your heart what to say to each girl. The Bible tells us to love one another and to build each other up in the faith. What you say tonight may show a girl in this room something God has done in her life that she may not realize. Tonight is not a time to bring up faults or negative things. There is a time and place for those difficult discussions, but that is not what this affirmation time is about."

Allow each girl to sit silently in the affirmation chair and instruct each person to take a turn affirming her. You may want to start the affirmation each time a new girl sits down. You know your girls and the personality and dynamics of the group. They may need a jump-start the first time you do this, but they will soon catch on—which may result in your having to cut off the time in the end! You may want to let them know about the affirmation time a week in advance so they can get their thoughts together about each girl.

Another option for a small group is to design a page for each girl and allow the girls to write a note of affirmation on every girl's sheet but their own. You can design this on the computer and make it unique for your group. Printing the sheets on cardstock will make the sheets more durable. This kind of affirmation is a little more light-hearted and the girls can laugh, talk, and eat while writing. You can string ribbon through the top and even laminate the pages so the girls can hang their affirmation page on a doorknob, their mirror, or the wall. I attached a magnet to the back of mine to hang on the refrigerator so I see it often.

✿ **Large group:** If you have a larger group, you will want to set up the room a little differently. You will need to consider the time as well. In this case, each girl will affirm each other one-on-one, not one at a time. (We had fifteen girls in a group with three leaders, and affirmation went well into the night.) Soft music and candles still soften the atmosphere. Start off with Scripture, prayer, and explanation of what you will do. Give the ground rules and explain the process. This is a little more complicated, but once the girls get the idea, it will be easy. Divide the girls into two lines, facing each other. Choose one girl who is standing at the beginning of her line to start. She will walk to the girl directly in front of her and be affirmed. Then, she will turn around and walk to the girl who is now at the beginning of the other line. After being affirmed, she will turn around and walk across to the other line. At this point, the girl who first affirmed her will follow her through the line. A girl will continue zig-zagging between the two rows until she runs out of fellow group members. Then she will stand still and affirm the girls who are making their way between the two rows, being affirmed. Confused? See the diagram on the next page. Each letter represents a girl.

AFFIRMATION SERVICE · CHART FOR LARGE GROUP

BEGINNING

```
A          F     B
G
C          H
D          I
E          J
```
Girls stand in two parallel lines, facing in toward each other.

ROUND 1
```
          A → F
B         G
C         H
D         I
E         J
```
Girl A walks across to Girl F, who says encouraging words to Girl A.

ROUND 2
```
          F
B → A     G
C         H
D         I
E         J
```
Girl A now turns and walks to Girl B, who encourages her.

ROUND 3
```
B ← F   A → G
C         H
D         I
E         J
```
Girl A walks across to Girl G and is encouraged. Girl F starts and goes to Girl B to be affirmed.

ROUND 4
```
B        F → G
C ← A     H
D         I
E         J
```
Girl F moves on to Girl G, while Girl A moves onto Girl C.

ROUND 5
```
          B → G
C ← F   A → H
D         I
E         J
```
Girl B now joins in, walking across to Girl G. Other girls being affirmed continue to make their way through the lines by zig-zagging back and forth.

ROUND 6
```
              G
C ← B   F → H
D ← A     I
E         J
```

ROUND 7
```
C ← G   B → H
D ← F   A → I
E         J
```

ROUND 8
```
C        G → H
D ← B   F → I
E ← A     J
```

ROUND 9
```
          C → H
D ← G   B → I
E ← F   A → J
```

ROUND 10
```
              H
D ← C   G → I
E ← B   F → J
A
```
Now that A has run out of people, she assumes her new position next to Girl E and prepares to encourage Girl F.

ROUND 11
```
D → H   C → I
E ← G   B → J
A ← F
```

ROUND 12
```
D        H → I
E ← C   G → J
A ← B     F
```

ROUND 13
```
          D → I
E ← H   C → J
A ← G   B → F
```

ROUND 14
```
              I
E ← D   H → J
A ← C   G → F
B
```

ROUND 15
```
E ← I   D → J
A ← H   C → F
B → G
```

ROUND 16
```
E        I → J
A ← D   H → F
B ← C     G
```

ROUND 17
```
          E → J
A ← I   D → F
B ← H   C → G
```

ROUND 18
```
              J
A ← E   I → F
B ← D   H → G
C
```

ROUND 19
```
A → J   E → F
B ← I   D → G
C ← H
```

ROUND 20
```
A        J → F
B ← E   I → G
C ← D     H
```

ROUND 21
```
A          F
B → J   E → G
C ← I   D → H
```

ROUND 22
```
A          F
B        J → G
C ← E   I → H
D
```

ROUND 23
```
A          F
B         G
C ← J   E → H
D ← I
```

ROUND 24
```
A          F
B         G
C        J → H
D ← E     I
```

ROUND 25
```
A          F
B         G
C          H
D ← J   E → I
```

ROUND 26
```
A          F
B         G
C          H
D        J → I
E
```

ROUND 27
```
A          F
B         G
C          H
D          I
E → J
```
E affirms J. If J were to take her position across from E, you'd see that the girls are back in the same positions as when the activity began.

You may set up chairs, if you like, and have the girls stand behind them so that when the girls begin to make their way through the lines, they can sit down and be affirmed by the girl positioned behind that chair. However, you will be responsible for moving the chairs to the end of the row as girls move throughout the group and down the line. Or the girls can stand up and do their affirmation face-to-face or while embracing each other. Give girls a time limit for each affirmation, maybe a minute or two, depending on the depth of the bond between your girls, and then tell them to move to the next girl. When girls have returned to their original places, then the affirmation time will end.

Affirmation can be a spiritual marker and even a rite of passage each girl will look forward to every year. In seventh grade, affirmation may be a little awkward for the girls, but by the time they become seniors in high school, it will be a time they look forward to with great anticipation. Senior affirmation is a very special time that the girls will look back on and remember for a lifetime.

Communication has certainly changed during the last decade, which means we must adapt our methods of communication to teenage girls. Hopefully, these ideas will lead you to re-evaluate your means of communication with the girls in your church and that you will find current and relevant ways to communicate to girls the message of Christ.

CHAPTER 2

Ideas that Teach Spiritual Truths

O TEACH SPIRITUAL TRUTHS, Jesus used objects and ideas that people could understand easily. Think about the parables Jesus told and the opportunities in which He used sheep, water, wineskins, fish, coins, nets, and even leprosy. Jesus lived as an example for us by teaching people about God and His kingdom using things they readily knew and understood. It only makes sense for us to use things teenage girls know to teach them about the amazing love of Jesus Christ and His redemptive plan for their lives.

God's Word never changes and His truth will remain the same forever, but the methods we use to reach each generation must change to reach an ever-changing culture. The needs of girls are the same as they were when I was a teenager, but there are temptations, stresses, and issues unique to each generation. We must minister to each generation of girls according to those needs. The girls of the iGeneration are becoming teens now, but the latter members of the iGeneration are yet to be born. These girls have never lived (or will never have lived) in a world without cell phones, text messaging, the Internet, or iPods®. My 5-year-old granddaughter is a fluent iPod user and thinks nothing of it. She plays games on the computer and knows how to operate it in a way that I have yet to accomplish. My 3-year-old twin grandsons love Wii™ sports. They play golf on the Nintendo® and are very good. I am amazed they are so adept at something that their MiMi can't even comprehend. This just illustrates the world in which they live—a world that I cannot fully comprehend.

Staying in touch with teen culture and the complications each generation faces will equip you to design a relevant girls' ministry so you can effectively disciple teenage girls as followers of Jesus Christ. I do not encourage girls to read secular magazines that cater to teens, but I do encourage women to look through teen magazines from time to time so they can see the things that interest and involve teenage girls. Utilizing those interests to teach spiritual truths is an important part of girls' ministry. However, you need to be discerning in the activities you plan for the girls. You would never want to compromise the Word of God in an effort to be relevant.

If you are in your twenties, you will find it easier to keep up with teen culture. If you are older, you'll need additional help in deciphering what is going on with technology, music styles, and ministry styles. Whatever your age, surround yourself with women who represent different generations. I have years of experience in youth ministry and understand how parents think and what their needs are. I can relate to girls' ministry volunteer leaders. I have experience in church processes and wisdom gained from life experiences. On the other hand, I lack knowledge and understanding about how the postmodern generation and the iGeneration think. I need help keeping up with fast-paced technology and other rapidly-changing concepts. I need help from the younger generation, so I surround myself with younger women who are in touch with youth culture. I make lunch appointments and gravitate to these younger women. I ask questions and listen when they answer. I take to heart what they say, and I learn. I use that information to design ministry to meet the girls' needs. I also talk to teenage girls and let them know that I care about their lives. I ask them questions and involve them in ministry planning and decisions. If you and I don't pay attention, we will try to fit the younger generation into our mold, which feels awkward and doesn't work.

CREATIVE WAYS TO GET THEM THINKING

The ideas in this chapter are simply that—ideas. They need to be developed to fit the needs of girls in your church and community. These ideas can be used to teach spiritual truths to teenage girls in your church, home, or small groups. Involve the girls when developing ideas for ministry.

✿ **Teen magazine discussion starter:** Tear out pages from popular teen girl magazines. Look for pictures or text that either illustrate or contradict biblical principles. Distribute pictures or articles to girls and ask them to evaluate. Ask them to think about what the Bible has to say about the content of the picture or article. Teach the girls how to search in the concordance of their Bibles or on the Internet to find verses that would apply to the pictures or articles in the magazine. Listen respectfully to the girls' opinions, but guide them to discover truth from God's Word. Don't bash the magazine; simply teach girls how to evaluate the truthfulness of the content. Girls need to begin to filter the media they read through the lens of Scripture. Pray for God's Spirit to interpret that truth in their hearts and minds. Everything in a teen magazine is not bad, but teaching girls how to be discerning and measure the things they read against God's Word is an important life skill for a Christian.

A few years ago, our former pastor's wife said something that I will never forget, "You don't have to show teenagers a crooked stick, you only have to show them a straight one." It is important to teach girls how to think through ideas and information they are exposed to every day and determine if it is truth. You could use this idea as a springboard for discussing Romans 12:1-2; 1 Corinthians 6:18-20; or even Proverbs 3:5-6.

Our convictions will change as we learn more of His Word and what absolute truth means. Our preferences will change with the wind, but absolute truth never changes.

When girls are trying to make life decisions, encourage them to ask three questions:
1. What does the Bible say about this topic or situation?
2. What does the law say about this topic or situation?
3. What are possible results if I make this decision?

Their decisions should be made based on absolute truth, personal convictions, and personal preference. Dr. Don Wilton, my pastor, teaches this concept often. The Bible is absolute truth. It is our first place to consult when making decisions. Personal convictions are our values and how we interpret what we believe about the Bible. Our personal preferences are related to our tastes and what we like. Our convictions will change as we learn more of His Word and what absolute truth means. Our preferences will change with the wind, but absolute truth never changes. Absolute truth should never be compromised.

✿ **Self-defense class:** Teenage girls live with the faulty, grandiose, and egocentric idea that, "It will never happen to me." They are often distracted with text messaging, going to the mall, jogging with their iPods, plans for Friday night, and countless other things in the midst of a dangerous and evil world. Protecting themselves against a predator isn't even on their radar. Planning a self-defense class for teenage girls is a great way to make girls aware of the very real dangers around them.

Just outside of the student center of the downtown church where I am the girls' minister, a young woman closed her coffee shop late one evening, walked down the street alone and unaware to her car. She opened the door of her car and was shoved into the passenger seat at knifepoint by a man who appeared out of the shadows. He raped her repeatedly before she finally escaped after stabbing him in the groin with his own knife. It is truly a miracle she is alive. She fought furiously for her life, but she has since closed her coffee shop and lives with those tragic memories every day. The man was captured and convicted, but this young woman's life will never be the same. Teenage girls need to know how to prevent this kind of attack. They also need to know what to do in case they are attacked, and they need to know what to do if they are blessed enough to survive an attack. The following steps will help you plan a fun but informative self-defense class for the girls in your church:

1. *Enlist someone from your church or community who is trained in self-defense.* For the class at our church, we used the chief of police at a local college campus. He was also a black belt in karate and had a great sense of humor. He made the class informative with a list of do's and don'ts for the girls, but he also interspersed his instruction with self-defense techniques. He gave the girls funny sayings that helped them remember the techniques.

2. *Advertise the event well.* Get the girls to invite their friends. Send out a Facebook invitation or e-vite.

3. *Involve key girls in the planning.* Make the event fun and relevant.

4. *If you are in a small church, you can plan one event for seventh through twelfth grade girls.* If you are in a larger church, it might be a good idea to separate middle school girls and high school girls. When a girl begins to drive, there is a greater danger of being attacked, and they need a deeper level of instruction.

Here are some points to emphasize:

- *There is safety in numbers.* Don't go out alone at night if at all possible.
- *Always be aware of your surroundings.* Don't get distracted with text messaging, talking on your cell, or digging in your purse for your keys. Always have your keys in your hand before you leave the building for your car. Position a key between your index and middle finger and use it as a weapon if someone tries to attack you. Aim for the soft spot in the front of the neck with as much force as you can muster and twist. Repeat the action as necessary. (In class one girl squealed, "Oooohhh, I hate blood!" The instructor replied, "It is better to see your attacker's blood than yours.")
- *Jogging with your headphones in both ears is not wise.* Use only one side so you can hear what is going on around you.
- *Park in well-lit areas.* Look in your car before getting in it. Always lock your car when you get out and when you get in it.
- *Don't walk on dark streets at night*—even if you are with a friend.
- *In the animal kingdom, animals always attack weaker animals.* It is the same with people. An attacker is looking for an easy victim. Don't look like a victim. Hold your head up, walk with confidence, don't be distracted, and scream your head off if someone approaches you.
- *Trust your instincts.* Don't worry about being polite to strangers approaching you. Scream, run, or draw attention in any way you can. Being polite is important, but never trust a stranger who is approaching you on foot or even in a car. Never walk up to a car that stops beside you even if the person looks nice. Simply walk or run away, and scream if necessary.
- *Teach girls sensitive areas to target if they are attacked:* soft spot in the neck, eyes, groin, knees, toes, and so forth.
- *An important decision must be made if you are ever attacked:* to submit or fight. If you decide to fight, you must fight with every ounce of energy and brains you have.
- *Date rape is another danger posed to teenage and college girls.* Discuss ways to prevent date rape, such as avoiding parties with drinking and drugs. Never leave a drink unattended and then go back to drink it. (Someone could put a drug in it.) Never go to a secluded area alone with a guy, even if you think you know him. Don't be embarrassed to say no to his sexual advances and don't be afraid to scream. That's why God gave girls vocal cords that make a shrill noise; He knew we would probably need help to protect ourselves.
- *If you are attacked and are blessed enough to escape, get help as soon as you can.* Don't take a shower or bath. Go straight to the emergency room or police department. DNA evidence is very important in catching and convicting the attacker. Don't blame yourself; just get help.

When we hosted this event, we had a great response. Many mothers called to thank us for providing this training for their precious daughters. We even had mothers and girls' ministry leaders asking us to plan a second event. Evil abounds in the world today, and girls need to know how to flee. Often we teach our girls to be polite to everyone, putting them in danger of being a victim of the evil in our world. They need to know the difference in being kind and loving to others and how to protect themselves from evil.

Scripture offers lots of verses that teach of God's hatred of evil and His protection for those who love Him. You could use Scripture such as Psalm 5; 7; 10; and 11. Proverbs is full of verses on being wise and trusting in God.

This class is not meant to cause girls to live in fear but to be wise in their actions and trust God. Proverbs 10:27 says, "The fear of the LORD prolongs life, but the years of the wicked are cut short." We want our girls to live as long as possible and enjoy the full and abundant life God has planned for them.

Let's face it. The average teenager doesn't know much about etiquette and good manners.

✿ **Etiquette luncheon:** Let's face it. The average teenager doesn't know much about etiquette and good manners. (Lots of adults don't either!) Showing basic respect and courtesy is one of the basics of the Christian life. It's all about showing honor for others, God, and yourself. Somehow in our busy lives, we have neglected the challenge of teaching our children good manners. For smaller churches, an etiquette luncheon or event can be done in someone's home. Enlist a woman who is knowledgeable about etiquette to teach the girls. You may want to set the table with china and all the eating utensils for the meal. As the girls come to the table, you can teach them on which side of the chair to sit and which to exit, what to do with their napkins, how to cut their food, which eating utensil to use, and so on. You can walk them through the meal, giving instructions as they progress.

For larger churches, you may want to use the fellowship or dining hall of your church and invite older ladies to set the tables with their personal china. Each table would have a different theme and décor. The girls love this! Whether you have 5 girls or 500 girls, make it special and plan with excellence.

Teaching girls the proper way to respond to an invitation and how to write thank-you notes, as well as cell phone, e-mail, and text messaging etiquette are also necessary lessons for the iGeneration. Manners and etiquette are all about respect and honor toward others. Scriptures you may use for this event might include 1 Thessalonians 4:12 and 1 Peter 2:17.

✿ **Fashion show:** Girls love seeing the latest fashions and knowing what is in style. This event can be a great way to help girls know how to dress modestly and how to put outfits together to get more from their wardrobe. Often businesses will provide the clothes for a fashion show as a way of promoting their store. If you are fortunate enough to have someone in your church who is in the clothing business, he or she may be a resource as well.

You will want to monitor the clothes that are shown so you will not give the wrong messages to the girls. Some store owners may have a different idea of modesty than you want to convey to the girls! Consider using girls in your church to model the clothing. You can also do a "what not to wear" segment and show the girls styles that do not go well with their body types. (You might choose to use mannequins for this portion so you will not embarrass any of the girls.)

If you are in a smaller church, you might want to join with other churches for this event and promote it in your surrounding area. But you can also do this event with 15 or 20 girls and have a great time. Remember, plan with excellence no matter how many girls you have in attendance. Scriptures to include as a Bible study are 1 Timothy 2:9 and 1 Corinthians 6:19.

✿ **Scrapbooking:** Girls love to take pictures of their friends and themselves. Many girls post the pictures on Facebook, which is fine, but you may want to encourage them to preserve their pictures so they will have a permanent memory that they can look at anytime, anywhere. Gathering as a group on a yearly basis to create and maintain a girls' ministry scrapbook is a fun thing to do as well. Scrapbook each event you have for the girls. A spiritual journey scrapbook with pictures and journal pages of spiritual markers in their life is also a great idea for girls. They may want to keep a scrapbook of their journey through the youth group—keeping pictures of their mission trips, discipleship group activities, camps, retreats, and fun events. If the girls in your group enjoy this activity, you can do it on a weekly or monthly basis at someone's house or at the church. You can enlist a scrapbooking expert to provide the necessary materials and the girls can pay $5 to cover them, or they can bring their own materials.

Scrapbooking is a lasting memory that they will treasure even into their adult years. Using acid-free materials will keep their memories preserved for years to come. Girls in this generation don't often think of the importance of preserving their memories because they live in such a high tech, disposable world, so scrapbooking is a great activity to encourage them to keep records of their memories to pass down as a legacy of their faith. You can use Titus 2 to connect Scripture with the activity. It teaches women to pass down a legacy to younger women. Having a written record of what God is doing in their lives as they grow up will be a valuable tool in teaching their daughters, granddaughters, and younger women in general.

Girls in this generation don't often think of the importance of preserving their memories because they live in such a high tech, disposable world.

SPA EVENTS

Most girls like to look pretty and be pampered. A spa event can include foot massages, pedicures, manicures, make-up classes, facials, or anything that normal spas would offer. Look through teen magazines to get catchy, contemporary themes for your event. The following are some themes and the spiritual truths we emphasized:

✿ **"Color me perfect" or "All about you"**: Some girls have a drawer full of make-up and a closet full of clothes, but they can't seem to find the right look for their hair color, body size, and complexion. And perhaps their personalities could use a make-over as well. Girls can learn their personality types and how to respond to others in a way that will strengthen their relationships. This should be a fun-filled evening learning how to choose the right make-up and clothes and how to get along with friends.

This event can be held as an evening event (or even a sleep-over) at someone's home or an all-day event at your church. Enlist beauty consultants or women who are experts in the field of make-up and color to come and teach the girls how to choose and apply make-up. As they teach, encourage them to talk about inner beauty as well as outer beauty. Enlist someone to come and talk about fashion, body types, color, and modesty. If someone in your church or community is knowledgeable about the four personality types, enlist them to come and teach the girls about their personalities. A good resource for teaching about personalities is *Wired That Way* (Gospel Light Publications, 2006) by Marita Littauer. For more information check out *www.classervices.com*. The Bible study for teen girls, *Esther: The Role of a Lifetime* (LifeWay Press, 2008), could be used as a basis for this study. Esther used her beauty to influence a nation for good.

✿ **"Treat Your Feet" or "Beautiful Feet Pajama Party":** In our promotions, we said: "Do you want to have beautiful feet? Pedicures are a great way to pamper yourself and make your feet beautiful, but they are also expensive. Come and bring your friends to learn how to do your own pedicure or even how to do a pedicure for your friends. This spend-the-night party at_____ will be an incredibly fun night!" (Don't forget to include all the details: where, when, what to bring, what time it is over the next day, etc.)

Prepare devotions about feet, possibly using verses like Romans 10:15 and Psalm 40:2. You may also want to talk about our footsteps and where they've been and are going. Another idea is to talk about our footsteps and how younger girls are following in them. Where are we leading them?

✿ **Manicure Sleep Over:** You can also use the same idea as above, but adapt it for hands. Enlist someone to teach the girls how to take care of their hands with lotion, sun protection, nail files, cuticle oil, and polish (which kind of polish and remover are best, etc). Provide nail kits for each girl or have them bring their own. (Be careful in sharing nail tools between girls to prevent the spread of germs.) The devotion should be focused on our hands and how we use them, for example:
We can have beautifully manicured hands, but if we use our hands to hurt others, they are not truly beautiful. How do we use our hands? To send gossipy text messages? To make ugly signs to people we don't like? To physically hurt others? To write messages that say mean things about someone else? Or do we use our hands to help others? To send text messages to encourage others? To write prayers for others? To comfort those who are hurting? To make a meal for someone who is hungry? To do random acts of kindness? (Scripture to use would include: Psalm 24:4; Proverb 10:4; 31:20; 1 Timothy 2:8; and Ecclesiastes 9:10.)

CHAPTER 3

Creative Prayer Ideas

*T*EACHING TEENAGE GIRLS how to pray is one of the basics of discipleship, but keeping their attention focused on prayer is difficult. Countless things pull at their attention, and many girls never experience a moment in their day with complete silence. Often girls will watch TV, listen to their iPod in one ear, send a text message, and do research on the Internet all at the same time. This generation is certainly adept at multitasking, but doing all of those things while praying is counterproductive to cultivating a deeper spiritual life. God desires our undivided attention, but often teenage girls can't seem to focus long enough to pray.

It is easy to forget the potential of prayer in a teenage girl's life. Prayer not only leads to a closer relationship with Jesus Christ but could change their lives completely. When girls begin to communicate with Jesus and read His Word, He will speak into their lives with His transforming power.

One of the disciples asked of Jesus in Luke 11:1, "Lord, teach us to pray." That follower of Jesus could have asked for anything, but he wanted to know how to pray. Believe it or not, deep down in their hearts, teenage girls really want to know how to pray, too. One night in a small group of senior girls I had been meeting with for three years, I challenged them to pray for thirty minutes daily and to journal what God said to them while they were praying. You can imagine the "deer in the headlights" look I got from these girls who were busy with school, prom, grades, sports, preparing for college, and everything else that a girl goes through her senior year of high school. They were speechless for a moment, and then the rebuttals began. "We can't pray for five minutes, much less thirty minutes! What do we say for thirty minutes? When will we find the time to do this with all the homework and other things we have going on?"

Despite their objections, I didn't back down. After all, the girls had signed a commitment as a group to do whatever it took to become a disciple of Jesus. We had talked about prayer many times, and I had encouraged them to pray on a daily basis but had never challenged them to pray for thirty minutes every day. Those twelve girls left my house that night thinking it would never happen. To be honest, I doubted they had been praying all along and didn't know if they would start now, but I thought anything was better than nothing.

The next week they came with journals in hand, bubbling over with excitement. They couldn't wait to get eating out of the way so they could discuss what had happened in their lives. I was amazed at the things the girls had written in their journals. One girl who has ADD and whom I never expected to be able to focus on anything for thirty minutes was the first to speak. She said, "When I got started, I couldn't stop. I kept talking to God, and then I kept thinking of more things to say to Him. Before I knew it, I had prayed for an hour!"

This generation is certainly adept at multitasking, but doing all of those things while praying is counterproductive to cultivating a deeper spiritual life. God desires our undivided attention, but often teenage girls can't seem to focus long enough to pray.

The next week, I received a mid-morning call from this same girl saying she needed to come to my office immediately. She had called her mother for an early dismissal from school, and her mother was so shocked at the reason that she consented. The girl walked into my office red-nosed and puffy-eyed. The night before, while she was praying, God had spoken to her. She was living a double life and hanging out with friends who were influencing her to drink alcohol. God had spoken. She needed to stop this lifestyle and separate herself from these friends. I advised her to go back to her friends and tell them what had happened in her life through prayer. I encouraged her to tell them she was drawing a line and would no longer be involved in their lifestyle. I told her to invite her friends to come on this side of the line with her. If they chose to stay on the other side of the line, she should let them know she would not continue to be influenced by them. It was their choice at this point if they would remain friends. Not only did God work in her life in an incredible way, but He also worked in the lives of the other girls in the group. Their senior year was a time of great preparation for their college years, and most of those girls are serving the Lord today as they graduate from college.

Not every girl is willing to sit in her bedroom and pray for thirty minutes to an hour a day, but this generation of girls will respond to creative prayer times. Engaging and interactive prayer seems to be more appealing to the iGeneration. Because this generation of teens responds well to interactive and visual activities, it is important to teach girls how to pray in creative ways.

PRAYER IN YOUR SMALL GROUP

The following prayer ideas are designed for group prayer or private prayer times at home. Be creative and take the ideas below and modify them to fit the girls in your church or community.

✿ **Small group prayer times:** If you meet with a group of girls on a regular basis, you may want to purchase inexpensive prayer journals for the girls to use when they share prayer requests. They can decorate the front of their journals and write down the prayer requests and pray at home each week for the other girls. They can also write their prayer requests on index cards; each girl chooses a card and prays for a specific girl during the week. Encourage the girls to put the card in a place they will see it often, such as their mirror at home, their locker at school, or even on their on the sun visor in their car. If it is a personal request that no one else should see, it should be kept in a private place. The girls can also write in code if need be. A text message or call letting a girl know she's being prayed for can be the encouragement that gets her through the week.

✿ **PowerPoint® guided prayer:** PowerPoint or other multimedia presentations can be used to guide groups of girls to pray for specific things. Put each prayer topic on a different slide along with verses, pictures, or photos of people or groups who need prayer. Gather girls for a special time of prayer with a journal and worship music playing along with the presentation (if you have that capability). Make sure you allow enough time per slide for girls to process and reflect on what is being presented. Things you may want to put on the slides include:

- Pray for God to reveal His presence to you now.
- Thank God for one way He has demonstrated His love for you recently.
- Pray for God to draw you close to Him.
- Take time to write about your love for God. Worship Him with your words in your journal now.
- Ask God to show you things in your life He wants to change. Write those things in your journal as God speaks. Confess your sins to Him.
- Thank God for His grace and forgiveness and fresh starts.
- Thank God for the good things in your life.
- Pray for three lost friends you don't want to go to heaven without.
- Pray for our church.
- Pray for the youth pastor, your discipleship leader, your Sunday School teacher, and the pastor.
- Pray for your mom and dad.
- Pray for your brothers, sisters, and other close family members.
- Ask God to show you if there is anything you should ask forgiveness for from another person.

Keeping her prayers in a journal to present to her husband on their wedding night along with her True Love Waits ring will be a special gift.

✿ **True Love Waits prayer journal:** Encourage each girl to keep a prayer journal for her future husband. She probably has no idea at this point in her life whom she will marry, but God knows. Keeping a journal of prayers for that person will help a girl guard her heart and help keep her pure through her teen years. God will answer prayers in protecting that person, keeping him pure, and preparing him to be the husband and parent he needs to be in the future. Journaling prayers will guide a girl in setting standards for dating. It will not only be a blessing in her life but for her future husband as well. Revelation 5:8 tells us that God keeps our prayers in golden bowls full of incense. How important our prayers are to Him! Keeping her prayers in a journal to present to her husband on their wedding night along with her True Love Waits ring will be a special gift.

✿ **Prayer stations or centers:** Set up prayer stations, each with a different focus. Centers can be set up on tables or on the floor in a large room. When school starts each year, we set up a prayer station for each school represented in our church. We gather pictures of students or print words on colored paper that represent students or groups from that school. With worship music playing in the background, girls go to each center and pray for the people and things that are represented. You could also invite parents to join you for this special prayer time.

You may want to set up prayer stations for a special girls' event or emphasis. For example, before a conference or retreat, set up prayer stations at a time when the girls are already meeting. You could set up stations for the speaker, the band, the girls who will come, salvation for any girl who is unsaved, and other aspects of the conference. If possible, provide a visual reference (such as a picture) or something tangible to help the girls focus and prevent their minds from wandering while they are praying. Use color, design, and pictures to attract the girls' attention.

✿ **Facebook prayer groups:** Setting up a prayer group on Facebook is an appealing way to engage girls in prayer. Put a prayer thought or emphasis and Scripture on Facebook each day or week and invite girls to pray individually for the needs. This will help guide girls in their prayer life. Ground rules should be set up requiring girls to put only their own personal requests online (and not the personal requests of others). It is important to monitor the group to make sure requests are prayed for and that nothing inappropriate is added as a prayer request.

PRAYER WALKING

Teaching girls to prayer walk can be an eye-opener for girls to see the power of God. Prayer walking can be done in neighborhoods, around schools, churches, hospitals, or any place where people need prayer. Encouraging and teaching girls to pray as they walk can help them understand in a tangible way how to pray without ceasing.

The purpose of prayer walking is to talk with God, focus on Him, and pray for specific persons, groups, or purposes. Encouraging girls to prayer walk personally or in groups will cause their relationship to be deeper with God and with one another. When girls are praying together for specific purposes, the bond between them will grow deeper. When they begin to see God answer their prayers and focus completely on Him, their relationship with Him will grow deeper. Prayer walking should never draw attention to the person or group. It is a personal conversation with God. The following ideas for prayer walking are easy to implement:

Prayer walking should never draw attention to the person or group. It is a personal conversation with God.

✿ **Back-to-school prayer walking:** Girls can meet on the school campus to prayer walk before school starts each year. Assign each girl a specific thing to pray for, such as: teachers, school administrators, students, coaches, protection of students physically and spiritually, for God's Spirit to surround the campus and draw students, teachers and administrators to Himself, and so forth. The girls can meet at a specific location and then spread out and walk the campus individually if it is a safe area. The girls can walk together and pray, but sometimes it is hard for girls to be quiet and focus if they are together. Give them specific guidelines on where they should walk and a specific time to meet. Then meet back at the designated location and pray together.

✿ **Prayer walking for a person who is sick:** When a girl in our youth group had cancer, the students in our ministry would prayer walk in her neighborhood and even in the yard around her house. Groups would also meet in her yard to pray together for her healing and that God would use her illness for His glory. God answered those prayers in a mighty way. After Hannah passed away, a ministry to cancer patients was begun in her memory. Hannah's hope and faith in Christ are now reaching all over the United States.

✿ **Mission trips for the purpose of prayer walking:** You may also take girls to a foreign country for the sole purpose of prayer walking. This may be a country in which mission work and evangelism are not permitted. It is important to train the girls and to have someone with the group who knows the country, culture, and laws. You never want to put your girls in danger, but this can be an incredible opportunity for missions.

I once heard of a group that went to a country where Christianity and evangelism were not permitted. A doctor happened to be in the group, and as they were prayer walking, a man ran up to the group and said, "My son is very sick! Can you help him?" The doctor actually saved the boy's life and led the man and his family to the Lord. Was this a coincidence? I don't think so. I believe God led the man to the group, and He answered the prayers of this group.

✿ **Prayer walking around your church:** Encouraging girls to prayer walk your church building(s) for certain purposes and times in the life of your church will help them feel involved and connected with the larger church body. They may prayer walk before a girls' ministry event or student ministry event, a revival, a difficult business meeting, and so forth. You can meet at a certain time and walk together or assign girls a specific time to be there and prayer walk. Instruct girls to walk and pray for the specific areas where certain aspects of the event will happen (worship, Bible study, meals, baptisms, etc.). They can walk and pray over every seat, at the altar area, where the speaker will stand, where the band will perform or music will happen, or over the media area. Sometimes technical difficulties can throw the focus off of God, so praying for the media and technical areas is always important. Teaching girls to prayer walk can be life-changing for them and can change the lives of countless others. The Bible commands us to pray in many different passages, including: 2 Chronicles 7:14; Matthew 5:44; 6:5; Luke 6:28; Mark 11:24; 1 Thessalonians 5:17; and James 5:13. Prayer walking is a perfect way to introduce teen girls to an active prayer life.

OTHER PRAYER IDEAS

✿ **Breath prayer:** This is also known as "the cry of the heart." It can be used any time, anywhere. In this practice, girls sit quietly for a few moments. Then they close their eyes and imagine Jesus sitting across from them, asking them the question, "What do you want Me to do for you?" Girls will continue to sit quietly for a moment and allow the answer to surface from their hearts. It should be something they deeply desire or need God to do for them—not for a friend, not for a family member. It should also be something beyond the superficial needs of their daily lives—

grades, boyfriend troubles, and so forth. Challenge girls to focus on their deepest desires, things within their hearts that they might not share with another person. It is something they feel a deep urge or yearning for. This is the cry of the heart.

Once they have determined that deep desire for God to work in a specific area, they should shorten that desire into one sentence. For example, if a girl just moved to town and is feeling lonely, she might say, "Be close to me." Or if a girl is fighting with a particular temptation, she might pray, "Give me strength."

Once girls have determined the sentence, they should choose a name for God that is particularly meaningful for them, such as Father, Shepherd, Lord Jesus, and so forth. Then, the girls should begin the prayer with this name of God and complete the sentence with their heart's cry. So the breath prayer might become, "Emmanuel, be close to me" or "Mighty God, give me strength." Girls should sit in silence and say the name of God as they inhale. As they exhale, they should offer their petition. Inhale: "Mighty God," exhale: "give me strength." As they sit still in the quiet of the moment, girls can slow down their minds and hearts to sincerely reflect on the meaning of God's name they have chosen and listen to the prayer they are offering to God.

As they sit still in the quiet of the moment, girls can slow down their minds and hearts to sincerely reflect on the meaning of God's name they have chosen and listen to the prayer they are offering to God.

This prayer can be prayed during a daily quiet time before God, or at any time the thought or need arises: in the shower, while driving, when tired, while talking on the phone, in the midst of an unsettling situation, when facing a temptation, and so forth. It is a great way for girls to remember that God is actively involved in their lives and cares deeply about the deep concerns and needs in their hearts.

✿ **God and me:** This prayer experience is a little different. To do this, give girls a piece of paper and some markers, paint, or colored pencils. They should sit in the quiet for a few minutes and reflect on their relationship with God. Then, using the art elements provided, the girls should draw a picture representing how they see themselves and God. Girls should not focus on getting it right or perfect. They should draw out what they are thinking and feeling. If a girl feels small before God, she could draw herself as a tiny stick figure and God as huge. If she is feeling particularly close to God, she could draw herself as being held in God's hands.

Once the picture is drawn, girls should then explain the picture to God much like a child would explain a picture to an adult. Girls should talk about what they drew and why they drew it. They should then ask themselves the question: If God were to draw a picture of us, what would He draw? If time allows, girls could draw that picture. It is a great way to allow God to speak to girls through an artistic medium.

✿ **Letters from God:** Many girls keep a prayer journal, but this type of journaling is a little different. They should write out their prayer to God as they normally would in a journal, telling God what they are thinking and feeling, good and bad. They should be honest before God and pour out their hearts to Him about what is going on in their hearts and lives, the big stuff and the little things. Then, girls should skip a line and write "Dear _____" (girl's name). They should sit quietly and wait for God to speak to their hearts. They should then compose a letter back to themselves as if God were writing to them. It is amazing to see how God speaks to girls as they reflect on their prayers, listen to God, and wait for Him to speak truth into their lives.

If girls are not facing an acute crisis or needing to pour out their hearts before God, then you can choose to do this activity by focusing on one aspect of their spiritual lives. Topics could include:

- A particular sin with which I struggle
- How I've seen God take care of me lately
- A person or group with a great need
- What I want to be like ten years from now
- My secret ambition

Again, girls should be honest before God and tell Him everything about the particular topic. And again, girls should skip a line, write their "Dear _____," and then allow God to speak to them about what He would say in response to their journal entry.

CHAPTER 4

Bible Study for Girls

I LEARNED MANY YEARS AGO not to assume anything when working with teens. J.T. was a seventh grader, and I encouraged him to go to youth camp with us. When we were ready to leave, I noticed he was not among the names on the list. The Sunday after youth camp ended, I saw J.T. in Sunday School. I told him how much we missed him and how sorry I was that he had not gone with us. He replied, "I hate sleeping in tents outside!" He was very disappointed when he found that we stayed in a nice resort. I assumed that J.T. knew what camp was like, and as a result, he missed an important opportunity in his life.

Recently, the student minister at my church started his message during our student worship time on Wednesday night by asking, "Is the Bible relevant to your life?" Dead silence. He asked again, "Is the Bible relevant to your life as a teenager?" Still, no answer. Finally, he asked, "Do you know what *relevant* means?" This time a chorus of voices answered, "NO!"

It is easy to assume that teenage girls know the Bible and how it applies to their lives, but often that is not the case—even if a girl has grown up in the church. Studying the Bible in small groups and teaching them to apply it to their lives are both foundational in girls' ministry. The Bible is their handbook for navigating the teen years and ultimately life as an adult. It is relevant to their daily lives and has the answers to their problems.

Often we teach what the Bible says, but we fail to teach how it applies to their lives. I am happy to see more and more Bible studies written especially for teen girls that help them discover how the Bible is relevant.

Bible study for teen girls is best accomplished in small groups, whether it happens in Sunday School, discipleship groups, or even a group that meets in a home. Discussion is easier and more personal, and you can build relationships more easily in small groups. If you are in a small church and have only a few girls in your group, you can still carry out an effective Bible study. You simply start with the girls who come and study the Bible with them.

Since Bible study is best accomplished in smaller groups, the organization and administration for larger churches is more complicated. It will take a greater effort to find leaders, organize girls into groups, and decide what each group will study. I will devote the entire next chapter to small group discipleship and Bible study to help you accomplish this goal.

LEADING FOR TRANSFORMATION

When leading girls in small group Bible study, your goal is moving them toward spiritual transformation, not the mere transmission of facts. The following tips were adapted from the article "Tips for Making Spiritual Transformation a Reality Through Bible Study" by Sherry Spillman, Student Ministry Specialist at LifeWay Christian Resources.

1. *Make sure the meat of the Bible study actually searches Scripture, is spent in examining God's Word,* and is not just a discussion of girls' and leaders' opinions or beliefs. It is only by having hands on God's Word that girls will discover real truth.

2. *Be careful not to answer your own questions.* Give girls time to think when you pose a thought-provoking question. Let girls know that the silence that follows your question is OK. When we answer our own questions, we teach girls that they do not have to respond and that their answer probably was not important anyway.

3. *Work toward using activities that lead girls to discover the truth for themselves.* When we lead them to discover truths out of God's Word instead of telling them what we know, we allow opportunity for the Spirit to do His work. As we pair girls up or put them in groups to complete an activity, the Holy Spirit makes the truth relevant to each of their individual lives. He is freed up to do this when girls are allowed to dialogue about the assignment and God's Word and steer it where they need it to go, contingent upon what is going on in their lives.

4. *Watch for those times that the Holy Spirit makes Himself known within the session.* Those times, very frequently, take place as girls share results of their group work or report on their findings in the Word. Be ready to help girls make connections with God during those times.

5. *Prepare your heart for worship to take place during the Bible study.*
When we think of worship, we traditionally define it by the hour set aside
for "worship" identified by the components we normally experience
(i.e. several choruses, drama, solo presentations, and exhortation or
preaching.) Real worship takes place any time we come face to face
with God and leave His presence transformed or changed. So in reality,
worship should take place in our Bible studies. Sometimes girls will say
things that are totally profound. When God grabs your heart as that
happens, be transparent and let your girls know that you just had a
connection with God.

6. *Make sure that your girls are given an opportunity to measure their own
lives against the truth you have studied.* When they take the time to
examine their lives, compare themselves to a Holy God, realize that they
fall short, and make a commitment to surrender to Him, true worship has
taken place.

RESOURCES FOR BIBLE STUDY

As a general rule, we know the importance of Bible study. Sometimes,
though, we as leaders don't know what is available. The rest of this
chapter will be devoted to some of the recent Bible studies that have been
published specifically for teen girls.

*Give girls time to think when you pose a thought-provoking question.
Let girls know that the silence that follows your question is OK.*

✿ **CONFIDENT** (*LifeWay Press, 2009*): Culture encourages girls to find their
confidence in external sources—social status, popularity, having the right
clothes, the right hairstyle, and the right boyfriend. The problem with all
of these things is that they are temporary. A girl can go from the "It Girl"
to a social outcast in a matter of minutes. Clothing and hairstyles change
overnight. Boyfriends come and go. This Bible study challenges the world's
notion by explaining a girl's only true source of confidence—her Creator. It
will examine how sin has affected a girl's God-given confidence and how
Christ came to restore that confidence. It will help girls discover a different
way to live their lives—the way God intended when He created them.
Written by Carol Sallee, well-known speaker and author.

✿ **WOVEN: A RETREAT FOR TEEN GIRLS** *(LifeWay Press, 2009)*: Nothing is more powerful than a united group of believers. Nothing is more destructive than a divided group. This five-session DiscipleNow-style retreat Bible study will help your group examine elements of unity, destructive forces that come against it, the damaging effects of exclusive groups, and the importance of the body of Christ working together. This retreat-in-a-box contains everything needed to lead a group of girls. It contains ten student books, leader materials, and a CD-ROM with lots of extras, including T-shirt templates, PowerPoint® presentations, publicity materials, and supplemental teaching ideas for big budgets, small budgets, and everything in between.

✿ **GIRL TALK: THE POWER OF YOUR WORDS** *(LifeWay Press, 2009)*: Gossip. Lying. Crude jokes. Cursing. Sexual innuendoes via text messaging (called "sexting"). This resource tackles a major issue for teen girls—their speech. Girls will learn that life and death are in the power of the tongue (Prov. 18:21). Written in a DiscipleNow format (suitable for a retreat or a weekly study with no homework), this five-session Bible study contains a student book and a leader's guide. Written by Pam Gibbs, a veteran of student ministry and Girls' Ministry Specialist at LifeWay Christian Resources.

✿ **ESTHER: THE ROLE OF A LIFETIME** *(LifeWay Press, 2008)*: We're drawn into "once upon a time" followed by passion, intrigue, and danger. We love it when the good guy wins and they all live happily ever after. We get swept away by car chases, love triangles, mistaken identity, and the triumph of good over evil. The story of Esther can sweep you away, too (except there's no car chase).

There is a king and queen. There is a good guy (and girl!) and a bad guy. A murder plot. A beauty pageant. You'll find suspicion. Intrigue. Danger. And a surprise ending. By the end of this study, teen girls will be swept up in a story of one woman who chooses the road of courage and action, changing the course of her nation's history. Girls will also discover that even though God may be silent, He is not absent. He is always working.

This book also contains leader material for small groups, so teens can learn about Esther with their friends. Together, they'll see God working not only in Esther's life, but also in their own. Each week contains quizzes, learning activities, quotes from teen girls, and journal starters. Written by Pam Gibbs.

✿ **INSIDER** (*LifeWay Press, 2008*): What if you could give teen girls a tool that could change the way they relate to the opposite gender now and in the future? That is the focus of this girls' Bible study. Based on the book *For Young Women Only*, written by Shaunti Feldhahn and Lisa A. Rice, *Insider: What Guys are Thinking and Why You Need to Know* gives girls a glimpse into what's really going on with guys. Combining research with biblical truth, this study gives girls practical principles for relating to guys. With these tools, teen girls can develop better relationships now and build a foundation for the future.

The student book is a magazine containing over 300 photographs and illustrations. It also contains quizzes, devotional material, an advice column, and tons of other features, like articles written from guys' perspectives and features quotes and opinions from the guys themselves. The DVD contains teaching segments featuring authors Shaunti Feldhahn and Lisa A. Rice, along with introductions and wrap-ups from Christian recording artist Britt Nicole. Also featured are interviews with teen guys who spoke on camera about the topics in each week's study—a big hit with teen girls.

When we lead them to discover truths out of God's Word instead of telling them what we know, we allow opportunity for the Spirit to do His work.

✿ **HANNAH'S ONE WISH** (*LifeWay Press, 2008*): Misunderstood. Dismissed. Yearning. Taunted. Faithful. Hopeful. This is Hannah's story. Through this study of an amazing biblical character, teen girls will be able to embrace Hannah's story as their own. They will wrestle with God's sovereignty, recognize areas of their lives they just can't change, discover how to respond when the wicked prosper, and learn that it's not about them—it's all about God. This study is designed for teen girls to take small chunks at a time, digest them, and learn from a woman who lived thousands of years ago and yet struggled with the same issues they do. Also included in this Bible study are stories from teen girls who faced similar issues as Hannah, so girls can get a glimpse of how others have dealt with struggles in an honest yet trusting way.

This book contains leader material, so girls can learn about Hannah with their friends in small groups. Together, they'll discover the hope and peace that come from trusting God—no matter what life throws at them. Written by Kelly Minter, an author, worship leader, and speaker to young women.

✿ **HIS GIRL: A BIBLE STUDY FOR TEEN GIRLS** (*LifeWay Press, 2006*): This eight-week interactive Bible study is designed to look like a teen magazine. It is aimed at helping girls discover biblical truths to guide them through adolescence and beyond in an ungodly world. Topics such as conformity, true self esteem, purity, modesty, boys, and girl politics are discussed in a way that is appealing to girls through articles, quizzes, advice columns, and more. In addition to the student book, there is a leader's guide and DVD pack with videos featuring other teen girls speaking from their hearts regarding issues they face on a daily basis. It is based on the book *Your Girl* by best-selling author Vicki Courtney.

✿ **WILD ABOUT YOU** (*LifeWay Press, 2006*): This resource, adapted from Angela Thomas' book *Do You Think I'm Beautiful?*, is aimed at helping teen girls recognize their value as a child of God. This Bible study is designed to look like a magazine and help teen girls understand that God pursues them passionately because He loves them deeply. It will also help them recognize false loves and lies that lure them away from a devoted relationship with God. In the end, it will challenge teen girls to celebrate and live in the freedom of knowing and believing in the unshakable and unquenchable love of God. A DVD pack is also available with teaching segments from Angela Thomas and video interviews with BarlowGirl. The video was filmed in New York City and will appeal to teen girls.

✿ **RADIANT: DISCOVERING BEAUTY FROM THE INSIDE OUT** (*New Hope Publishers, 2007*): This six-week Bible study is written to help teen girls radiate their unparalleled beauty as found only in Jesus. Contains journal spaces, Bible study activities, meditation, and prayer starters. A leader's guide is also available. Written by Chandra Peele.

✿ **LIFE STYLE: REAL PERSPECTIVES FROM RADICAL WOMEN IN THE BIBLE** (*New Hope Publishers, 2006*): Teen girls today are hit with a dizzying array of lifestyle choices, all of which can seem tempting. They need all the wisdom the Bible offers to help them become godly women. This twelve-week study focuses on a different woman of the Bible each week to address issues such as identity, self-worth, body image, eating disorders, and dating. Each week, girls will learn a memory verse to help them hide God's Word in their hearts. Written by Whitney Prosperi.

✿ **A DAUGHTER'S WORTH: A BIBLE STUDY FOR TEENAGED GIRLS** (*Tate Publishing, 2006*): This is a twelve-week, interactive Bible study and devotional. Each weekly topic deals with modern struggles, many of them uniquely female (self-worth, emotions, and dating, for example). Although teens can use this book for daily devotions, a group study enables them to share thoughts and gain insight from an adult leader. Before gathering each week to discuss a specific topic, girls complete five brief devotions which include Scripture, application, journaling, and prayer. At the conclusion of each devotion, additional prompts encourage seasoned believers to dig deeper. Written by Ava Sturgeon.

✿ **TRUST: SURRENDERING TO GOD AND LEARNING TO FORGIVE** (*Regal Press, 2006*): This study discusses the power of surrendering your life to God. It challenges girls to trust Him with their hopes and dreams and to authentically follow Christ. Short prayers, Scripture, and questions for reflection are included. Small group ideas are also included. Written by Tamie Vervoorn.

We should never forget that our ultimate goal is to encourage girls to rely on the Bible as truth and learn to apply it to their lives.

Of course, the greatest book we can offer teen girls is the **Bible**. At my church, we offer many choices for small groups to study in our girls' ministry. Not long ago one of the leaders asked, "Is it OK to just use the Bible as our Bible study in discipleship?" I was floored that she even felt she had to ask. It drew me back to the point that you should never assume anything in ministry. As a result, we added "Holy Bible" to our choice of Bible study books. We should never forget that our ultimate goal is to encourage girls to rely on the Bible as truth and learn to apply it to their lives. As you encourage and expose girls to Scripture on a regular basis, they will begin to realize its relevance to their lives.

CHAPTER 5

Ideas for Small Group Discipleship and Mentoring

IN APRIL 2006, one of the key student leaders in the church where I serve was diagnosed with a rare and aggressive form of cancer. Hannah was getting ready to enter her senior year of high school when she was diagnosed with sarcoma, and her life and death were a true inspiration to people who knew her. Hannah was faithful to the Lord in her life and trusted in Him with a faith like I had never seen. She was a strong Christian young woman and believed until her last breath that the Lord Jesus would heal her, and on November 6, 2006, He did just that. As Hannah lay in her living room surrounded by her family and discipleship group, she left this earth and was ushered into the presence of God completely healed and whole.

Three days before Hannah passed into eternity, I was scheduled to travel to Nashville, Tennessee, to teach a girls' ministry class at the National Women's Ministry Forum at LifeWay. I was torn as to whether I should go or not since the doctors had told Hannah's parents that her life was nearing its end. I called Hannah to let her know that I was supposed to be away to teach. She was insistent that I go and gave me a message for the women I would teach. I share Hannah's message every opportunity I am given:

"Mrs. Jimmie, you **have** to go to LifeWay and tell those ladies there to go back to their churches and start discipleship groups. Being in a discipleship group for almost five and a half years has helped me make it through the past six months of my life. My relationship with the Lord, the love and prayer support I have from the girls in my group, and my leader have helped me stay strong during my illness. My relationship with the Lord is strong because my leader taught me how to study the Bible and pray. She taught me how to love the Lord with all my heart. The girls in my discipleship group have been with me all the way. Tell those women that discipleship groups are the most important thing they can do for the girls in their churches."

Hannah went to be with the Lord while I was teaching at the forum, but I know I was exactly where she wanted me to be. It was amazing to see what God did in the lives of the girls in Hannah's discipleship group. I watched them faithfully stay beside her bed and faithfully pray for God to work through Hannah's illness. The shallow things that are normally important to high school girls no longer mattered. They looked at life through eternal eyes, and I am proud to say they are still walking closely with the Lord in their lives today. When they come home from college, they always get together, and they pray for each other even while away at school.

Discipleship groups (called "D-groups" in our church) are important in the lives of teenage girls. Not only do small groups help to meet the relationship needs a girl has, but they also give her a place to belong. When structured and led properly, girls will grow close to one another and close to the Lord. If you don't already have discipleship groups set up in your church, you can find tips for structuring them in the *Girls' Ministry Handbook*, available for purchase online at *www.lifeway.com*. This chapter will be devoted to creative ideas to use after groups are already established.

Not only do small groups help to meet the relationship needs a girl has, but they also give her a place to belong.

One important issue that was mentioned in the *Girls' Ministry Handbook* is worth mentioning again: girls' ministry is different than women's ministry because it involves minors. There are specific laws governing what you can and cannot do when minors are involved. There are also certain laws that require you to report situations in which abuse has occurred or is suspected. It is important to know the laws of your state and have a child protection policy in place for your entire church. This policy will govern how anyone under 18 years of age is treated in your church and who is allowed to lead or be with minors. It is always important to have at least two adults leading one discipleship group. In our church, we have two adults working with no more than ten girls. This way, each leader is responsible for caring for and keeping up with five girls. It is up to these leaders to select their group's curriculum (from a list of books we provide) to use in their weekly meetings, which take place on Sunday nights in homes all over the city.

DISCIPLESHIP GROUP IDEAS

Once the groups are formed, you can carry out ministry, outreach, fellowship, and other aspects of community life in creative ways. Listed below are some ideas you may want use or adapt to meet the needs of your group.

✿ **D-Group baskets or bags:** At the beginning of each discipleship year, you can purchase baskets or bags and fill them with things the girls will need for discipleship groups. Your church's budget will determine what you are able to purchase for the baskets. Some options are pens, highlighters, colored pencils, prayer journals, study Bibles, praise and worship CDs, devotion books, and so forth. LifeWay publishes *ec magazine*, which features daily devotions and articles for students. Consider purchasing a bulk subscription for your youth group and distributing them via these baskets or bags. You might want to give each group a basket with one or two things at the beginning of the term and add items at intervals throughout the year. Stores or businesses may donate some items or at least let you purchase them at a reduced rate.

✿ **Discipleship scrapbook:** Girls love to take pictures, so you may want to have a night occasionally when you meet together and scrapbook the memories for your discipleship group. Special nights like Reach Night (discussed later in this chapter), Christmas get-togethers, mission trips, birthdays, and other special occasions are all opportunities to take pictures. You can make one scrapbook for the entire group, but the girls will probably want their own scrapbook to keep. Inviting someone to teach the girls scrapbooking is a fun thing to do as well. Creative Memories or other scrapbooking consultants are always happy to come and teach, but be careful about allowing them to sell supplies during that time. You may allow them to give out their business cards, but make sure the girls don't feel pressured to purchase supplies that night. Of course, the girls may need to pay $5 or so to cover the supplies.

✿ **Facebook D-group:** You can form a group for your discipleship group on Facebook and chat back and forth, send messages to the group, and post pictures and Scripture verses for the day or week. You have control over who is accepted into this group and of course, you only want the girls in your group to join the Facebook group. This makes the bond more special and entices girls who are not in a discipleship group to join.

✿ **Gift Bibles:** One discipleship leader, who started with a group of 7th grade girls and continued with them until they graduated, purchased a Bible for each girl. Each week she underlined the verses they studied and wrote notes in the margins of each Bible. Her group was small, so this was not a burdensome task. But she was very disciplined and continued to write in their Bibles for six years. When they graduated, she set aside a special night, invited their parents, affirmed each girl, and presented her with the Bible she had underlined for them. This was a priceless treasure to those girls from a very special adult in their lives.

✿ **Prayer Calendar:** One discipleship leader created a prayer calendar on her computer so the girls were praying for the same thing on the same day. For example, on Day 1 they prayed for a specific girl. On Day 2 they prayed for a different girl. On another day they prayed for specific things for the group or their church, their leader, etc. She placed a different Scripture for each day and a short thought for the day. This took time on her part, but the girls appreciated the effort, and they held each other accountable for their prayer lives. She created a calendar page for each month.

DISCIPLESHIP GROUP EVENTS AND PROJECTS

✿ **Daughters of the King celebration:** Sometime during the junior or senior year, plan a special night where the girls dress up during their discipleship meeting time.

One D-leader planned a sit-down dinner for her girls. They dressed up in formal dresses, and the leader presented each girl with a special gift to signify that she is a daughter of the King. Some leaders give a special piece of jewelry, a framed Scripture card, or other inexpensive gift. Some of the girls used their prom dresses or borrowed a dress from a friend. One girl was not able to get a dress, so the other girls went on a crusade to find a dress for her. She normally did not wear make-up, so a couple of the girls met her early and helped her apply make-up and do her hair. This girl felt as beautiful on the outside as she always had been on the inside. The D-leader had someone there to take pictures of each girl and then the group. These were wonderful pictures to put in their D-group Scrapbook. Of course, the girls had a great time and made special memories.

Some groups ask the fathers to escort their daughters that night, depending on the dynamics of the group. If the fathers of the girls in your group are involved in their daughters' lives and would feel comfortable escorting them, it is a good idea. If several of the girls do not have fathers, it is probably better to only have the girls attend. This is a situation in which you need to know the dynamics of the girls in your group.

✿ **Reach Night:** If you think about Jesus and His twelve disciples, they were actually an exclusive group to some extent. There were times when only those thirteen men were together. They traveled together, ate together, prayed together, and ministered together. At times, others were not included in their small group, but there was never a time when they ignored a physical or spiritual need.

It is important for the discipleship group to be together to pray, learn, and hold each other accountable, but these groups can become cliquish and ignore the physical and spiritual needs of others.

In discipling teen girls, it is important for the discipleship group to be together to pray, learn, and hold each other accountable, but these groups can become cliquish and ignore the physical and spiritual needs of others. In order to give students an avenue to reach out to other students, we started having a Reach Night once a quarter. Each D-group chose an activity, and every girl in the group invited a girl who didn't attend church and possibly wasn't a believer. Prior to Reach Night, the discipleship leaders coached the D-group girls in conversational evangelism (how to share their testimony of what God means to them in a conversational way). Reach Night included a fun activity. (See the list below.) Nothing was mentioned about discipleship, but the girls were invited to attend Crossfire, which is our Wednesday night worship time for students, and Sunday School (which we call Life Groups) on Sunday morning. Listed below are some of the Reach Night activities the girls chose:

- Paint pottery, then go to dinner
- Fondue party
- Scrapbooking
- Spa party
- Bonfire with hot dogs and s'mores
- Capture the flag
- Girls' Fun Night: make-up and manicures (beauty consultants came to teach the girls how to apply make-up)
- Rock climbing and dinner at a restaurant
- Pizza party
- Personalize your journal cover (give your book a new look!)
- Scavenger hunt
- Game night
- Make your own pizza and cookies
- Progressive Dinner: appetizer, main course, dessert each in different homes
- Trip to a doughnut shop
- Cooking class
- Manicures and pedicures
- Watching a movie like *Left Behind* or *Facing the Giants*

When the girls who were invited to Reach Night accepted Christ, began attending church, and wanted to grow deeper in their relationship with the Lord, they were added to a D-group. Keep in mind that sometimes the groups become too large and must to be divided into two groups. When girls reach out to their friends, you will begin to see your girls' ministry and student ministry multiply. You may have to coach the girls on the importance of keeping those D-groups small. They may not like the idea of being split into smaller groups.

✿ **Adopt a Grandmother:** One of our groups adopted an elderly shut-in from our church. They did something special for her once a month, especially for holidays and special occasions. They made cards, sang songs, and had devotions with her. They made cookies, took small gifts, and enjoyed holiday meals with her. In turn, she shared stories, wisdom, and expertise with the girls. On one occasion, they planned a meal, shopped, cooked, and enjoyed the meal together. She used her fine china and even taught the girls etiquette and manners while they ate. They expected to make life happier for this elderly lady, but in turn, she blessed their lives tremendously. Even though these girls have graduated, they still keep in touch with their adopted grandmother.

They expected to make life happier for this elderly lady, but in turn, she blessed their lives tremendously.

Because our church is large, many of our girls' ministry activities and events are done through our discipleship groups. It is easier to manage a small group, so when we are participating in an event outside of our church, such as a conference or retreat, the discipleship leader is responsible for transporting her discipleship group to and from the event. We go caroling every Christmas as a youth group, but each D-group goes to a different place. In essence, the discipleship group leader is the youth minister for that small group under the direction of the girls' minister or student minister.

For smaller churches that may have one or two discipleship groups, planning and logistics are much easier. At the same time, it is important to plan with excellence and put as much effort into a small group of five girls as you would ten groups of five girls.

Mission Projects for Girls

MANY CHURCHES PLAN MISSION TRIPS or projects for their youth groups, but churches sometimes underestimate the potential of teenage girls in the area of missions. Girls have a nurturing bent that God gives to women and therefore have great potential when it comes to mission opportunities. However, even though females have the innate ability to nurture others, they are often egocentric and think only of themselves. More often than not, the girls in our churches are spoiled; they are unaware and unconcerned about the needs of people in other areas of their own towns, much less the rest of the United States or other countries. They have the skewed vision that the rest of the world is exactly like life in their neighborhood. Mission trips into needy areas at home and abroad will be life-changing. Giving teen girls a world vision for missions is important. Listed below are ideas you can develop to fit the personality and culture of the girls in your church:

✿ **Adopt a grandmother:** Several of our small groups have adopted a grandmother. The woman could be someone inside the church or someone who is in need but not a member of the church. You can get information regarding the names and needs of elderly women from your pastor or staff person responsible for caring for senior citizens. You might contact nursing homes or assisted living facilities in your area as well. Here are some steps to assure success:

1. Get in touch with the elderly person before you show up with a group of girls. Set up a day and time to visit. Then make sure you are there on time. It would be very disappointing for the grandmother if you make an appointment and then don't show up or are late.

2. Explain what the girls would like to do: bring a meal, rake her leaves, sing, or whatever project you would like to do initially. Ask your adopted grandmother what her needs are and how the girls can meet those needs. She may have a need that no one knows.

3. Train the girls before you go. Sometimes elderly people are hard of hearing, they may say or do things that are a little strange to the girls, their houses may smell a little musty or medicinal, and as a result, the girls may be a little apprehensive at first. Encourage the girls to be polite, talk with their new grandmother, and use their manners.

It may be necessary to visit and do projects several times to build up the trust of an elderly person. On the other hand, you will probably find her very welcoming, and she will want to do things for the girls in return. You will go with the intentions of blessing her, but she will probably be more of a blessing to the girls!

The iGeneration wants to be involved. They want to make a difference. They want to do hands-on missions and want to reach the world for Christ. They simply don't know how.

✿ **Christmas for others:** Every year at Christmas, we host a party for children whose families cannot afford to purchase Christmas gifts. The girls of your church can sponsor this event. It can be for one or two children, or if you belong to a larger church, it can be for a larger number of children. I would suggest you start small the first year and grow each year if you make this an annual event. You may know of a family in need, or you can go through the church office or school system to find a family who has a genuine need. The Christmas party can be held at your church and may involve games for the children, lunch, Christmas carols, the Christmas story, and opening gifts. You may or may not choose to have a Santa visit, depending on the convictions of your church and pastor. The main purpose is to bless the children and share the true meaning of Christmas. The girls can pool their money to buy presents for the children. At our church, two girls go in together and buy presents for one child. We set a limited amount of money to be spent so each child is treated equally. This mission event can be sponsored by your girls' ministry but can involve others as well, especially if it turns out to be a success.

✿ **Girls' home:** If you have a girls' home or children's home in your area, consider doing mission projects for the girls who live there. We have a children's shelter in our area, and the component of this shelter for teenage girls is called The Anchor House. The girls' discipleship groups from our church have adopted The Anchor House as their mission project. On Valentine's Day, each discipleship group made a basket for a girl there. We were invited to deliver the baskets to the girls, and they were overwhelmed at the demonstration of love and concern.

Because of the nature of the situations of girls at the shelter, the guidelines are very strict. Here are a few suggestions to follow in working with government agencies or even private children's facilities:

1. Call and make an appointment to talk with the director of the facility. Find out what their guidelines are and follow them. Make sure the girls from your church understand the guidelines and stress the importance of following them. This will determine whether you have a long-term relationship with the facility.
2. Find out the ages of the girls in the home and their needs.
3. Start early when doing a project. Give your girls plenty of time to gather things and develop their ideas. We started immediately after Christmas working on the baskets for Valentines. We gave each discipleship group a list of items to choose from to go into the basket.
4. You may or may not be permitted to lead devotions or share the gospel with the girls when you go. You can, however, add things in their basket like Christian CDs, Bibles, devotion books, and so forth. Your girls can write cards sharing their testimonies to add to the basket.

This kind of mission project can be done with children's homes, children's hospitals, nursing homes, or individuals. If you choose a mission project for a children's hospital, you may want to take a small gift for each child so everyone receives something. You never want to leave out any child. Often holidays are very sad for those who are in facilities of this type. Funds are limited for the holidays, and this can be an avenue for girls to spread the love of Jesus Christ with others in a tangible way.

✿ **ICU missions:** Having a family member in intensive care at the hospital can be a devastating and depressing time. It can also be financially straining for families. Often family members will sit in the ICU waiting room for hours or days with very little to eat except snacks from a vending machine. This presents an incredible ministry opportunity for the girls in your church; however, there are some steps to take before showing up at the hospital.

1. Call the hospital chaplain and get permission to begin this ministry.
2. Find out the rules and regulations from the hospital on what you are allowed to bring, when you are allowed to visit, and what you are allowed to talk about.
3. Set up a specific time once a week to visit the ICU to replenish snacks and drinks. Find out the best time to go. Most intensive care units have specific times set up when family members can go in to visit their loved ones during the day. You would not want to go during this time.
4. Train the girls. Talk to them about how a person feels when they have a sick or injured loved one. Teach them what to say and what not to say. You may want to have name tags for the girls with the church's name on them. If you add the girls' names, use only their first names. Never allow the girls to go alone to the hospital. Always have an adult with them for their safety and to guide their actions while there. They should never give their personal phone number to anyone. It is a good idea to give a business card from the church if a patient's family member has a specific need.
5. You can take individual drinks, individually wrapped snacks, homemade cookies, muffins, fruit, veggie trays, or anything that would be easy to eat in a hospital waiting room. Use disposable trays or containers to prevent extra clean up work for the hospital staff or people in the waiting room.
6. You may take devotion books, tracts, or any material your church has that would be comforting or helpful and place them in the waiting room. Sometimes just sitting and waiting is painful. If the person has something to occupy his or her mind, the waiting may be easier. This kind of reading will open their hearts and minds to allow God to speak to them.
7. The girls should go into the waiting room, set up the food, and then go to individuals sitting in the waiting room. They should give their first name, the name of your church, and say something like "We have brought some

food and drinks from our church. May I bring you something to drink or eat?" If the person declines, they can reply, "Feel free to help yourself later on if you get hungry." The girls can also ask, "What are your needs? Would it be okay if I pray for you right now?" Warn the girls not to probe into the person's personal life. Don't ask too many questions about what happened to the person in the hospital. Asking to pray for someone is also a good way to approach the person. The girl can sit beside or kneel in front of the person and pray for their needs. It is better to go to individuals or families sitting together as opposed to walking into the waiting room and making a general announcement and praying for the entire group. Some people would be embarrassed by this.

8. Direct the girls to always be polite and respectful. This is not a time to play around and laugh with each other. Their focus should be on ministering to people who are hurting.

Your girls will find this to be a very rewarding ministry. Often people will come to your church after their tragedy. Because you ministered to them in their time of need, they may feel an emotional connection to your church and desire to be involved in your church afterwards.

The most important part of setting up mission projects and getting girls involved is allowing them to come up with the ideas and take ownership of the projects.

✿ **Foreign mission trips:** Mission trips in foreign countries can be life-changing. Your church can organize and implement a foreign mission trip for teenage girls, their leaders, and even their families. The prospect of doing this may be as foreign to you as the country itself, but it can be an incredible, life-changing experience. If your church has a missions department, talk with the person in charge of this area. If you are in a smaller church and don't know where to start, you can contact the International Mission Board (IMB). The IMB provides training and opportunities for students to go on short-term mission trips. They will organize a trip for your girls' ministry, youth group, or even provide opportunities for one or two students to go with other groups. You can contact the IMB by going online to the Students on Mission Web page at *http://www.thetask.org/youth/YOM/yom.htm.*

❀ **Acteens:** A great opportunity to involve teenage girls in missions is through the Acteens program. Acteens is a missions organization for girls in grades 7-12 which provides an opportunity for teen girls to learn about missions, do hands-on missions projects, go on mission trips, pray for missions and missionaries, and give to mission causes, which in turn helps teen girls develop a missions lifestyle. To find out more information about Acteens and how to start an Acteens program in your church, go online to *www.acteens.com.*

We polled girls' ministry leaders from around the country to get their ideas and suggestions for outreach projects. They provided some great suggestions:

- "We collected used prom dresses from the girls to donate to an area high school for their special needs girls to select for their own prom."

- "A fun thing that I did this past August with a group of our stronger leader girls was to put a conference together that they led . . . We went to a small church in Alabama and these girls taught all the lessons, led fashion shows, led worship, shared testimonies, had game time, and were able to take all the things that they have learned/are learning and invest into the other girls from this church! We had a blast. We will be doing this again at a girls' home."

- "For Christmas, we got the names of girls who were at a group home. We purchased $1 stockings and put each of their names on a stocking in glitter paint. Then we filled the stockings with items such as candy, make-up, pens, pencils, etc. We also included a Christmas card and all signed our names. The total cost was no more than $10 per stocking. It was a huge hit!"

- "Our students usually use the VBS student curriculum for their Spring Retreat and then assist in our church's summer Vacation Bible School. After a couple years of doing this, the students weren't ready for VBS to be over. We now use all of the things we've gathered and take our VBS on the road. We use the lesson plans and curriculum to teach VBS in local parks in our community and in churches we work with on our Mexico mission trips."

• "Once every three months we have the opportunity to take a group of our girls down to the feed the homeless at a church downtown. They serve them, share with them, and help clean up the facilities. I truly wish that we had more opportunities like this!"

• "My small group is throwing a baby shower for a teenager with no family and no support system."

• "Our teenagers have begun serving in Honduras and other countries conducting VBS, assisting pharmacists, dentists, and medical staff and organizing and working folks through the process while evangelizing."

• "We make visits to fire and police stations with baked goods and cards and pray over their building. They always show us around, and the students really like seeing behind the scenes. Last time we went to the police station, they let us sit in the 911 call center and see all their 'toys.'" (Another group recently distributed the movie "Fireproof" to the local fire stations.)

• "We love taking our students to the Boys and Girls Club. We have played kickball with the kids there, worked on computer skills in the computer lab, and tutored in elementary math."

• "One of my favorites is a community garden that our youth help tend. We give 10 percent of our crops to our local food bank and give some of the remaining goods to families in need in our congregation."

• "We help workers at the local fair (commonly known as 'carnies'), one of the most neglected groups of people in our nation. Our students give them a small treat and thank them for bringing the fair to our community. Our adults provide a nice steak lunch, new pillows for them, a mobile dental health clinic, and immunizations for their children."

Here is a list of other ideas. Take them and run with them!

• Collecting blankets and sending them to those in need

• Nursing home visits—painting nails and doing other girly things for the elderly women there

• Reading to/mentoring school children

• Working on homes in low income housing (painting, scraping, installing new window screens)

- Partnering with other churches on mission projects

- Helping at an assisted living facility, doing everything from helping residents recover passwords on computers to cleaning out closets

- Serving at various meals and events at church

- Assisting in children's VBS and sports camps

- Baby-sitting at Parents' Night Out

- Assisting Special Olympics athletes at their events and cheering for them

- Working at safe house for abused mothers and children (painting, clean-up, baby-sitting, etc.)

- Sponsoring a ministry to unwed pregnant teen mothers, from baby showers to collecting clothing and food

- Developing a park ministry (with skits, music, and a complete worship program in place of the evening service)

- Sorting and organizing clothing/food pantries (for local residents in need)

- Disaster relief

- Participating in walk-a-thons to raise money for a school with special-needs children

- Picking up garbage during community trash pickup/adopt a street

- Cleaning up meth and drug houses in community

- Providing after-school sports programs

- Giving music lessons for younger kids

- Handing out free hot chocolate during Christmas parade

- Volunteering at local humane society

- Working at a halfway house for women recently released from prison

- Sponsoring a child from an impoverished nation (through an organization such as World Vision)

- Organizing a teacher appreciation meal at local schools

- Providing backpacks of food to children each Friday who may not eat on weekends when not in school

- Providing activity bags to be given out by emergency room nurses to children who are in the waiting room during a family emergency (includes small book, activity pad, pencil, crayon, stickers, etc.)

- Donating teddy bears to pediatric unit to be given to children who don't receive gifts, balloons, stuffed animals, and so forth

- Learning to knit as a group. Making baby caps, chemo caps, small finger puppets, scarves, and other things to donate to those in need.

- Collecting items for Easter baskets for inner-city kids

- Baking brownies for employees at the courthouse

- Collecting supplies or stuffed animals for an abuse shelter

Leading girls to have a global heart for missions is part of discipling them and growing them up to be godly women. The iGeneration has the greatest opportunity to complete the Great Commission than any past generation. Technology and the ease of world-wide travel provides access to unreached people groups, and the iGeneration wants to be involved. They want to make a difference. They want to do hands-on missions and want to reach the world for Christ. They simply don't know how. Your church can provide the resources and opportunities to make it happen. However, the most important part of setting up mission projects and getting girls involved is allowing them to come up with the ideas and take ownership of the projects. If they want to invest, they are much more likely to encourage their friends to get involved and really see change happen.

Rites of Passage and Other Events

RITES OF PASSAGE and celebrating spiritual milestones are an important part of growing girls up to be godly women. Often, we participate in or initiate rites of passage without realizing it. Christian ceremonies, training, and celebration are an important part of our lives as Christians and are often motivators for much of what we do. They give girls something to look forward to and provide precious memories.

According to Ginny Olson, in an article titled "Fish Guts and Pig Intestines: Rites of Passage for Adolescent Girls," a rite of passage in the broadest definition is "anything—a ceremony, decision, action—that moves someone from one stage in life to another."[1] There are many rites of passage that come and go without parents or churches recognizing what they actually mean: birthdays, graduating from kindergarten, graduating from middle school, accepting Christ (salvation), baptism, participating in the Lord's Supper for the first time, entering the youth group, getting a driver's license, going on a first date, becoming a teenager, starting menstruation, turning 16, going to prom, becoming a senior, graduating from high school, and entering college.

Ceremonies and celebrations are important to girls as they go through life, but often the church fails to make these rites of passage meaningful. Depending on your church, adolescent girls enter the youth group either in sixth or seventh grade. They are leaving the "little girl" stage and entering into womanhood. How do we celebrate or recognize this entrance into a new stage of life? In a larger scope, how can the church create meaningful rites of passage or celebrate spiritual milestones in the lives of teenage girls? What are the rites of passage we already recognize and celebrate, and how do we make them more meaningful spiritually? How do we plan meaningful events that grow girls up to be godly women?

MILESTONES

Recognizing special spiritual milestones in a girl's life is important. Listed below are questions and suggestions to encourage your thinking about how to celebrate special milestones in a girl's life.

✿ **Salvation:** How do you recognize a girl who has accepted Christ? Do you give her a special gift, send her a card, or recognize her in a special way? Does she go through a special class or training, and if so, how is she recognized when she has completed it? In our student ministry, we have a special youth baptismal service once a quarter for all students who have accepted Christ. We light a large candle at the front of the church and have smaller candles around it to represent each student being baptized. When a student wades into the baptismal waters, the student minister or pastor calls for family and friends to come to the front of the church and stand in support while the student is being baptized. A special person in that teen's life lights his or her candle. This is to show that he or she is willing to support that teen's Christian walk and to pray for that teen on a regular basis. After the baptism, the teen is given the candle to take home as a reminder of those family and friends who committed to support and pray for him or her. After the baptism service, we have a reception where family and friends celebrate the baptism and give words of blessing to every student that has been baptized. If a student is saved and wants to be baptized before the youth baptism service, we go ahead and baptize that student as they wish.

Ceremonies and celebrations are important to girls as they go through life, but often the church fails to recognize or to make these rites of passage meaningful to our girls.

✿ **Birthdays:** How do you recognize a girl's birthday? Do you mail a birthday card, send a message on Facebook, or give a small gift? If you are in a smaller church, it may be possible to purchase a small gift, but with a large girls' ministry, it may not be possible. Some computer programs that manage church membership can produce a list of birthdays to help you remember each girl's special day. Facebook also lists the upcoming and current birthdays of people on your friend list. It is easy to post a happy birthday wish to girls on Facebook, and there is no cost.

In our church, many of our D-groups celebrate birthdays of the girls in their groups. For example, the leader of one of our groups bakes a cake and prepares a special dinner for each girl in her group on that girl's birthday week. She has five girls in her group so it is not a huge task if done through small groups. The girls look forward to choosing their favorite meal for her to prepare. When they sit down to eat the meal, each person says a blessing over the birthday girl.

Christian ceremonies, training, and celebration are an important part of our lives as Christians and are often motivators for much of what we do. They give girls something to look forward to and provide precious memories.

❀ **Other Milestones:** Do you recognize girls when they have memorized Scripture, finished a certain Bible study, or completed a certain program? I remember as a teenager looking forward to the recognition services for finishing the steps in Acteens, a missions education program. That was a rite of passage, and I accomplished all the steps through Queen with a Scepter. I was cleaning the attic recently and found a box full of memories from that rite of passage. Mrs. Lankford, the Acteens director, always made sure it was a very special service. I remember walking down the aisle of the church in a white dress to receive the awards. It is a very precious memory to me to this day. Of course, the iGeneration girl might think that was a little old-fashioned, but the principle is the same. You can think of more up-to-date ways to recognize the girls in your church for their accomplishments.

CHECKLIST FOR EVENT PLANNING

Listed below are some important questions to ask when planning events or rites of passage for teen girls:

1. Who is your target audience? Middle school girls? Churched girls only? Girls outside the church as well? Girls and their moms? Girls and their dads?

2. What is the purpose, and what are you trying to accomplish with this event? (Build relationships through fellowship and fun, grow spiritually

through Bible study or training, recognize accomplishments or milestones through a rite of passage event, etc.)

3. What kind of event will it be? (Retreat, camp, sleep-over, conference, Bible study, recognition, prayer service, banquet, etc.)

4. Where will the event take place? (At the church? In someone's home? At a restaurant? At a retreat or conference center? Your budget will also factor into where your event will be held.)

5. How much will it cost? Will the church fund the event through the budget? Will you ask the girls to pay a registration fee? Doing a cost analysis is important in being a wise steward of God's money. This may determine where you will have the event, what gifts you give at the event, and what kind of food you have. (The *Girls' Ministry Handbook* explains how to set up a budget for a girls' ministry event. Events can be done with very little money from the budget of your church if done the right way and with a little creativity.)

6. When will you have the event? Once a year? During the month of the special milestone? Prior to the milestone? For every age group? Also, remember to check with the youth minister, women's minister, church calendar, and even local school calendars when planning events for your girls' ministry. You don't want to conflict with other events and force girls to choose between them.

In the next two chapters, we will discuss events for middle school girls and events for high school girls. In those chapters we will talk about events that can be considered rites of passage and how we can make those celebrations and events more meaningful and memorable in the lives of teenage girls.

If a girl has not had to wait for the appropriate stages of life, by the time she reaches her senior year, she has experienced everything and has nothing to anticipate.

Why would we separate rites of passage into two age groups? Often in a youth group, middle school girls do the same things and enjoy the same activities and special events as senior high girls. If a girl has not had to wait for the appropriate stages of life, by the time she reaches her senior year, she has experienced everything and has nothing to anticipate. Creating age-appropriate rites of passage or stages of participation creates a healthy pathway to becoming a mature young adult. It also prevents a girl from being rushed out of childhood too early and becoming bored with the normal things a teen girl should be enjoying. (As an example of the stages of participation, one church allows only seniors to participate in mission trips overseas. High school students go to another state, and middle school students stay within the state for missions work.)

The next two chapters will also talk about events that are not considered rites of passage but are productive and meaningful as well. Fasten your seat belts—it's a great ride! Girls' ministry is fun and the ideas are endless, but the greatest reward is when you see a girl come full circle in her life as a Christian young woman.

1. Olson, Ginny, "Fish Guts and Pig Intestines: Rites of Passage for Adolescent Girls," *Youth Worker Journal*, September/October, 2005. Available from the Internet: *http://www.youthspecialties.com/freeresources/articles/adolescent_development/fish_guts.php*.

CHAPTER 8

Middle School Girls' Rites of Passage and Other Events

INTENTIONAL AND ORGANIZED EVENTS and rites of passage are important in transitioning girls through the stages of becoming godly young women. Every event you plan for girls in your church should move them on toward maturity. Instead of girls moving from children's ministry to student ministry to college ministry unnoticed, it is important to design celebrations, training, and rituals that connect girls to God, one another, their families, and to the church. Their memories of moving into and through adolescence should be a positive experience (instead of a painful one), and the church can help make the transition memorable.

Before planning events for middle school girls, it is imperative to know their characteristics and developmental milestones. Middle school girls are experiencing changes in their bodies, their thinking, and in their likes and dislikes. They feel like they are on center stage and everyone is looking at them. (Psychologists call this an "imaginary audience.") They often feel like adults don't like them and are overly sensitive to comments made innocently by others. Their thinking is moving from concrete to abstract, and they are beginning to understand more about God and who He is in relationship to them. Middle school girls flip-flop from acting like little girls who want to play with dolls to the other extreme of wanting to be grown up, wear make-up, and show interest in boys. Sometimes it is hard to please them, and the most important relationships they have are with friends. Parents are not cool, and for the most part, girls are embarrassed to be seen with them in front of their friends. Many teenage girls would rather have their toenails pulled out by the roots than be seen on a Friday night hanging out with mom and dad at a restaurant or the mall.

Emotions run high and low with most teenage girls, and their moods can change quickly. A friend of mine recently drove her middle school daughter to school, a distance of about three miles. Her daughter screamed at her in anger, cried uncontrollably, and laughed hysterically all during the five minute ride, seemingly for no reason at all.

Research published by *TIME* magazine shows the prefrontal lobe of the adolescent brain is the last to develop. This is the reasoning center of the brain. Teens tend to rely more on the amygdala when making decisions, which is the emotional center and develops earlier than the prefrontal lobe. Adults tend to rely more on the prefrontal lobe when making decisions, which is the reasoning center. This may explain why preteens and teens tend to base decisions on their emotions rather than good sense and reasoning.[1]

You may look at the decisions of some teen girls in your girls' ministry and think, "What were you thinking?!" Probably, they were not thinking at all. Rather, they were making decisions based on their feelings, not using their prefrontal lobe of good judgment. It is important to remember this when dealing with teen girls. Teaching them to think and use their brain cells is important in developing their brains.

You may look at the decisions of some teen girls in your girls' ministry and think, "What were you thinking?!" Probably, they were not thinking at all.

IMPORTANT FACTORS FOR MIDDLE SCHOOL GIRLS

Listed below are some complications to remember about this generation of middle school girls, both in terms of ongoing ministry and special events and rites of practice:

✿ **Brain development:** As stated before, the prefrontal lobe of the brain develops later, so sometimes teen girls lack good judgment. They need guidance in thinking through and processing good decisions. In addition, the synapses in their brain are developing at a very rapid rate, much like they grow during infancy. As a result, all of that neural activity causes the brain to "short circuit," which results in many miscues, including a lack of confidence and depression.[2]

✿ **Acceleration of puberty:** Many girls begin puberty earlier than past generations. Marcia Herman-Giddens, an adjunct professor at the University of North Carolina's School of Public Health, noticed in her clinical work that more and more young girls were coming in with physical signs of puberty. She launched a study of 17,000 girls and the results showed the following: "Significant numbers of white girls—some 15%—were showing outward signs of incipient sexual maturity by age 8, and about 5% as early as 7. For African Americans, the statistics were even more startling. Fifteen percent were developing breasts or pubic hair by age 7, and almost half by age 8."[3] Her research was published in the journal *Pediatrics* before *TIME* did an article on it. Scientists and medical personnel are researching to discover a reason for this phenomenon. Whatever the reason, it is something we deal with in girls' ministry.

One of the results of this early onset of puberty is the sexual temptation teen girls must face. In earlier generations, girls would begin puberty later and would marry earlier. Therefore, they only had to deal with sexual temptation and strive for sexual purity for a few years. However, in this current generation, girls experience puberty earlier but marry much later. As a result, they must deal with sexual temptation and purity for a much longer time period. Add the overly-sexualized culture in which girls live, and it is no wonder many of them have serious struggles with maintaining their sexual purity.

The church needs to be intentional about bringing families together instead of assuming that families would create and guard those opportunities.

✿ **The family:** The breakdown of the family is another complication. Girls need rites of passage that connect them with family, such as mother-daughter and father-daughter events. The church needs to be intentional about bringing families together instead of assuming that families would create and guard those opportunities. Most of the time, the opposite is occurring. One parent is shuttling one child to an event while the other parent is shuttling another child in a different direction.

Training mothers and fathers how to love their daughters and meet their familial needs is another important aspect of girls' ministry. We cannot assume that they received that modeling in their own families as children. Many of them come from broken or dysfunctional homes themselves and need support, encouragement, and education in godly parenting.

✿ **Technology:** Rapidly-developing technology and instant communication resulting in more online relationships (rather than up-close and personal relationships) is another complication we need to consider when planning for girls' ministry. Girls can text but cannot carry on conversations in person. Corporations are struggling to find employees who can communicate well because of the surge of electronic forms of contact.

One of the downfalls of this technology and its impact on relationships is girls' lack of skills in learning to relate to the opposite gender in a healthy way. Boundaries are falling away as girls become more comfortable texting about issues they would never discuss in person. Masturbation, sexual prowess, and sexual experiences, which were once taboo to discuss aloud, much less in mixed company, are common topics of conversation electronically. Real conversations fail to take place as girls and guys merely text on the phone. They "go out" together but break up via text. Actual phone calls are rare, and as a result, some girls lack skills in expressing their thoughts and views. They struggle with this in general, but their culture of texting makes it even more difficult.

One of the downfalls of this technology and its impact on relationships is girls' lack of skills in learning to relate to the opposite gender in a healthy way.

✿ **Exposure to evil:** Girls are exposed to evil and more adult issues earlier because of technology and postmodern ideology. The commercials alone in an hour of prime-time television can expose a young girl to concepts, ideas, and content that should be reserved for adults—behind the bedroom door. This, combined with lack of good judgment and early sexual development, can be a combination for disaster. Girls have pieces of knowledge but have no skills or training to process or evaluate what they are seeing and hearing.

✿ **The need for interaction:** Middle school girls need to interact with concepts and with each other. They need experiential learning, not someone lecturing them. Although frustrating to those who work with them on a regular basis, girls are actually learning when they are talking to each other during Bible study. (But sometimes they're talking about boys!)

This need for interaction applies to adults as well. Often if a girl has a problem and comes to talk with you, she will discover the answer with a few thought-provoking questions and just a little bit of guidance from you. She just needed the face-to-face interaction and a little direction.

How do we design ministry for middle school girls that will transform them spiritually, help them become a more mature high school girl, and eventually become a godly, mature woman at the appropriate time? It takes a lot of prayer, a lot of thought about where middle schoolers are in the developmental stage, and intentional planning on the part of girls' ministry leaders.

Events that are simply fun usually take very little planning. You can take the girls to the mall, to the movies, out to eat, and have a sleep over, but how does that grow them up to be strong Christians? However, by thinking about the needs of middle school girls and planning purposeful and meaningful events, you can begin to design ministry that will meet the physical, emotional, intellectual, relational, and spiritual needs of the girls you are passionate about reaching.

EVENTS AND RITES OF PASSAGE

On the following pages are ideas for middle school girls' ministry. Again, you will need to take the ideas and adjust them to fit the needs of the girls in your group.

✿ **True Love Waits ring ceremony:** Making a commitment to purity is an important rite of passage for middle school students. True Love Waits is a student-focused international emphasis that utilizes positive peer pressure by encouraging students to make a commitment to refrain from sex until marriage and challenge their peers to do the same. (True Love Waits information and resources are available at *www.lifeway.com/TLW.*)

The True Love Waits emphasis is more common in the month of February (because of Valentine's Day), so that is when our church hosts its True Love Waits ring ceremony. We send out information to the parents of middle school students six weeks in advance. The parents are responsible for purchasing the ring, necklace, or other symbol for their son or daughter. It is open to any student, but most students choose to make this commitment early in their teen years. We conduct the ceremony after our True Love Waits emphasis in our youth group, when our student minister speaks for several weeks on sexual purity and the importance of making a commitment to purity. This gives the student an opportunity to make that commitment in their heart before the ceremony and not simply because their parents purchase a ring for them.

We have the ring ceremony in our chapel and make the evening special by decorating with candles and renting candelabras to have some resemblance of a wedding ceremony. In fact, this can be considered a pre-wedding ceremony in which the student makes vows before God, family, and friends to remain sexually abstinent until their wedding day when he or she will pledge fidelity in marriage. The program for the ceremony consists of the following:

- Welcome
- Opening prayer
- Special music: This can be a young person or someone the students admire. The music should focus on love and commitment, especially to God.
- Special message: You may choose a young person who has made the commitment or a couple who has successfully kept their commitment to purity to share their testimony. Be very careful about choosing someone who did not keep his or her vows as an example of what not to do. God is forgiving, but you never want to put someone in front of young people who might say something that gives students the idea that you can be sexually active and not reap the consequences. If a person has made mistakes in this area, always have him or her write out the testimony so you will know ahead of time what he or she will say. When you put a person in front of young people to give a testimony, you never want any surprises.

- Ring ceremony and vows: Parents come to the front, repeat vows to God and their son or daughter, and in turn their son or daughter repeats vows to God and parents. The parents place the ring or necklace on their child. (An sample ceremony and vows are available at *www.lifeway.com/TLW.*)
- Prayer of dedication (Parents place their arms around their child and pray a prayer of dedication over him or her.)
- Special music
- Closing comments
- Reception

Depending on the size of your group, one family at a time may say their vows, or if you have a large group of students, five or six families can participate at a time. This ceremony marks the commitment or decision of the student to live a life of purity and faithfulness to God. It is an important spiritual marker and rite of passage. This is a ceremony that parents appreciate and students remember for a lifetime.

The True Love Waits ring or necklace can be worn until an engagement ring comes along. Some girls choose to journal prayers for their future husband and place their TLW ring in a pocket in the front of their journal as a special gift to their husband on their wedding night. True Love Waits commitment cards are also available for students to sign and keep in their Bible as a reminder of their commitment if their parents choose not to purchase a piece of jewelry.

True Love Waits is a student-focused international emphasis that utilizes positive peer pressure by encouraging students to make a commitment to refrain from sex until marriage and challenge their peers to do the same.

✿ **Chic Chat** is a guided discussion time for middle school girls. You can name it anything you want, but the idea is to create time and space for girls to build relationships and engage in discussion. We have Chic Chat an hour before our Wednesday night youth group meeting during the summer months since parents are already bringing their girls to the church that day. (Adding an additional day for parents to transport their students may result in lower attendance.) Topics relevant to the lives of middle school girls are discussed, such as friendships, girl politics, boy relationships, self esteem, dressing appropriately, modesty, and current events. This kind of discussion helps girls to be open in their thoughts and feelings, but also helps them discover what God's Word says about these topics and how they should lead their lives as Christian young women.

If you have mature senior high or college girls who can lead these discussions, the middle school girls will look up to them and connect in a way they may not connect with older women. Often the younger women are more in tune with what is going on in the lives of middle school girls and know what topics to discuss. You may want to pair an older woman and a younger woman to lead the discussion.

It is also a good idea to provide snacks (especially healthy snacks of fruit, veggies, and dip). Girls are becoming more open to healthy foods if we offer them. Also bottled water is cheaper than sodas and much healthier. (Viewing your body as the temple of God and eating foods that promote good health and long lives would be a good topic for Chic Chat. I'm sure you can think of a more catchy title, but you get my point.)

Chic Chat can be a great relationship-building time, especially if you listen to the girls, respect their ideas, and then present the truth of God's Word on the issue. Sometimes, we as leaders have to hold our tongues, pray for the girls, and allow the Holy Spirit to convict their hearts after we have presented truth to them.

✿ **Sleep-overs:** Before they get a driver's license, girls are looking for ways to get out of the house. We can provide opportunities for healthy avenues of fellowship and being together. Inviting girls to come to your house on a Friday night is a great way to develop relationships. Making cookies, watching TV, sampling different make-up, experimenting with hair styles, trying on each other's clothes, and talking are great ways to build healthy relationships with the girls. Of course, your spiritual antennae should always be up, looking for girls who are hurting, having problems, or struggling in some area. Listening to conversations when girls are together is a great way to keep in touch with what is going on in their lives. Throwing in a devotional or guiding the conversation toward scriptural truth that applies to their lives is a great way to let them know they can have fun but also learn how the Bible applies to their lives.

✿ **Middle school girls retreat:** Getting away overnight for a girls' retreat can be a great opportunity to build deeper relationships with peers and with God. Taking a break from TV, the Internet, their cell phones, and the business and busyness of the world is important. A retreat provides the opportunity for girls to be alone with God in nature. Set up a time in which the girls go outside, sit, pray, and read their Bibles alone. There are numerous retreat centers and conference centers from which to choose, but cost is always a factor. You may have a church member who will open up his or her cabin or condo in the mountains, at the beach, or on a lake. Of course, advanced planning is required for food, sleeping arrangements, permission forms, adequate adult supervision, registration, fees, and programming. You may choose to use high school girls as counselors or small group discussion leaders. Make sure you train these girls on small group techniques and give them guidelines on what materials to use.

Make sure girls know what the rules are during the weekend. Do not overwhelm them with rules. One simple rule for a middle school girls' retreat is sufficient on your part—"Respect: respect God, respect yourself, respect authority, respect others, and respect property." Other rules may come from the retreat or conference center for the safety of the girls.

Make sure you provide some time to just hang out and talk. Girls need time to decompress from the pressures of their everyday lives.

Choose a theme and Bible verse for the retreat, as well as what you will teach. Depending on the size of your group, you may want to have large group sessions and smaller break-out groups. Middle school girls want lots of interaction, so make sure it is not all lecture and Bible study. Games, sports, and team-building activities that focus on the theme are all important when planning a retreat for middle school girls. And make sure you provide some time to just hang out and talk. Girls need time to decompress from the pressures of their everyday lives.

✿ **American Red Cross baby-sitting class**—Another rite of passage occurs when a girl moves from *needing* a baby-sitter to *becoming* a baby-sitter. This is an important life change for many girls. In today's world, most parents want their children left in the care of a teen who is responsible and has been trained in CPR and basic baby-sitting skills. The church can offer these classes through the American Red Cross. You can go online to *www. redcross.org* to find the closest chapter in your area. They offer baby-sitting classes at their local offices, or if you have a group of girls interested in the class, they may come to your church. It is an all-day class, usually lasting from 9 a.m. to 4 p.m. We ask the girls to bring a $5 bill (for pizza) along with a check made out to the American Red Cross for their class registration fee. (Keeping the food money and registration checks separate makes it easier.)

At the end of the class, I usually challenge the girls to picture baby-sitting as a ministry. They can show God's love and kindness to the children they baby-sit. They can take simple craft projects that will teach the children of God's love. They can take storybooks to read to the children about Jesus. I know of one young lady who baby-sat on a regular basis for a family who were not Christians. She read the children stories about Jesus and God's love for them. She prayed for them when they went to bed and taught them a blessing for their meal. Through her continued ministry to this family, the family members became Christians. A few months later, the entire family was killed in a plane crash. What a difference this girl made in this family's eternity!

✿ **Fun in the sun:** Girls like to hang out by the pool, so a swim party/Bible study summer event for middle school girls can be a great ministry tool. Recruit someone in your church who has a swimming pool or house on the lake to host the girls. Permission forms are important for this kind of event, and recruiting adults to supervise while the girls are swimming is essential. A mature high school or college girl can lead the devotion or Bible study. Plenty of food for hungry girls will top off the afternoon.

✿ **Girls' beach night:** In our girls' ministry, a trip to the beach is reserved as a rite of passage for senior high girls. In lieu of a beach trip, the middle school girls have a beach night held on our sand volleyball court at the church. Beach decorations, beach towels, umbrellas, lounge chairs, tiki lights, beach music, and other tropical accessories create the right environment. Inflatable swimming pools contribute to a fun atmosphere, and games such as water balloon volleyball, a limbo or hula hoop contest, and fruit smoothies all make this evening a fun event for the middle school girls. Recruit someone who plays guitar to lead the girls in praise and worship music and a devotion at the end of the evening.

BREAKOUT SESSIONS OR DISCUSSION TOPICS

The following ideas can be used for discussion topics with middle school girls at retreats, breakout sessions for conferences, Chic Chat, sleep-overs, or small group discipleship.

✿ **Fashion tips with Jen** (or someone the girls will think is cool and knows fashion): Jen owns a very modern clothing store close to our church. She is young, cute, and goes to New York to purchase the latest fashions. At the same time, she knows we are trying to teach the girls how to dress attractively, not seductively, and keeps that in mind when teaching. You may have a person in your church or area who would be willing to do the same. The following is the promotion we used to draw the girls:
"Keeping up with current fashions is an important part of looking your best. As Jen shops the market for the latest fashions for her boutique, she sees what's in and what's not. In this workshop, Jen will give you the most current fashions and coach you in choosing the styles and colors that are best for you individually. Jen will also teach you how to dress in the latest styles without compromising your integrity and modesty as a Christian young lady. This workshop will not only help you look your best, but it'll be fun as well."

✿ **Fun in food and fitness:** "Keeping your body healthy can be loads of fun. Eating right and being healthy shouldn't be boring. You can be creative in exercise and eating right. What does the Bible say about food and exercise? We'll examine Scripture during this workshop to teach you to have the very best body you can have as a teenage girl."

✿ **Express yourself!** "Come and see some of the coolest ways to decorate your bedroom. Learn how to make a statement about who you are and whose you are. You'll even learn how to coordinate bedrooms with your best friend to have rooms that look the same but are different. Plus, learn how to do it all on a budget."

✿ **When God's girl prays:** "Are the prayers of a teenage girl important to God? What happens when girls pray? The direction of your life can be changed when you learn to spend intimate time with God. The lives of your friends can be changed when you learn to pray for others. You'll even see some personal examples of how to keep a journal of prayers for your future husband."

✿ **Dealing with Daddy:** "Were you 'daddy's little girl' until you turned 13, when all of a sudden, you felt like a stranger around him? Maybe your dad doesn't quite know how to relate to his little girl-turned-young woman. Some dads are loving and kind, some are distant and uninvolved, some are harsh and abusive; nevertheless, we can learn to deal with our dads in a way that will bring out the best in them. How does your view of your dad affect the way you view God? It doesn't matter what kind of relationship you have with your dad, you will learn how to better deal with him."

✿ **Worship is more than a song:** "The word *worship* paints lots of different pictures. Worship is often seen as time during a service set aside for singing songs. This breakout session (or Bible study) will focus on what worship really means and how we can worship God in all areas of life. If you have a desire to develop a heart for worship, this is for you." (A great resource for this is *Live to Worship* by Rick Futch [LifeWay Press, 2008].)

✿ **Mean girls and me:** "Sugar and spice and all that's nice? Not always! It's tough to be a girl. Most girls will admit that they have been a mean girl or a victim of one at some point in their lives. Whether they're arguing about a boy, teasing a girl, or making up rumors, girls can be just plain ruthless. This workshop can help you end the cycle of meanness. In short, it's the answer girls need for the problem they never thought could go away." (A great resource to use is *Mean Girls: Facing Your Beauty Turned Beast* by Hayley DiMarco [Revell Books, 2008].)

✿ **Personality 411:** "Do you have a problem getting along with your friends? Are your parents always getting on your nerves? Do your brothers and sisters rub you the wrong way? Maybe it's just a personality conflict! Learning about the four personality types will help you respond to others according to their personality needs, and in turn they will respond to you in a better way. This is a fun workshop that will help you get along with others for a lifetime." This workshop can be built on Gary Smalley's four personality types—lion, otter, beaver, and golden retriever. For more information, see *www.smalleyonline.com*.

✿ **Make-up/skin care:** "Every girl needs help with her make-up from time to time. Taking care of your skin is important in your teen years. Using the right products, choosing the right colors, and applying the right amount will make a big difference. Learn the best look for you in this hands-on workshop."

✿ **What Do Guys Really Think?** What do guys really think about the things girls do—the way they dress, the way they talk or act, the way girls go after guys? Find out from a panel of guys exactly what the average guy thinks. You might be surprised! Don't miss this unique opportunity to hear from some of the most well-respected guys in our church. (Make sure you choose guys who will communicate Christian values.)

Middle school girls' ministry is a training ground for girls to become women. If we pour our lives into these girls and teach them intentionally through Bible study, special events, and rites of passage, then we will have a better chance of growing them up to be godly high school girls.

1. Claudia Wallis and Kristina Dell, "What Makes Teens Tick," *TIME* [online], 26 September 2008 [cited 7 January 2009]. Available from the Internet: *http://www.time.com/time/magazine/article/0,9171,994126-6,00.html*.

2. Melissa Trevathan and Sissy Goff, *Raising Girls* (Grand Rapids, MI: Zondervan, 2007), 72.

3. Michael D. Lemonick, "Teens Before Their Time," *TIME* [online], 30 October 2000 [cited 7 January 2009]. Available from the Internet: *http://www.time.com/time/printout/0,8816,998347,00.html*.

CHAPTER 9

Rites of Passage and Events for High School Girls

HIGH SCHOOL GIRLS' MINISTRY TAKES a major turn because the needs of high school girls are much different than the needs of middle school girls. Most high school girls have acquired a driver's license and have the ability to choose whether they attend an event at church. Dating is another factor. Most middle school girls are not permitted to date in a conventional way, but all of that changes in high school (for most girls). The focus and needs change overnight. Often high school girls are more mature in worldly ways and find the things that interest middle school girls to be juvenile and a waste of time.

Involving girls in planning ministry events is more important than ever in the high school years. Considering issues that are important to girls of this age will guide your planning. Many are in dating relationships, most are looking toward college, and some are focused on their sport or academics. Most have settled into their relationship with parents. Their relationship may be good, toxic, or nonexistent. Planning an event just to get girls out of the house and give them something to do probably won't fly with high school girls. They will only migrate toward an event or activity that fills a life or relationship need.

EVENTS AND RITES OF PASSAGE

A rite of passage for high school girls can be centered on salvation and baptism, entrance into high school, graduation from high school, getting a driver's license, becoming a senior in high school, and so on. These events can have deep spiritual meaning because girls usually understand the impact and depth of the milestone, especially when carried out with excellence. (Often middle school girls whiz through a rite without recognizing its significance.) The following events can be viewed as rites of passage for high school girls and can be adjusted to fit the needs of the girls in your church:

✿ **Driver's license recognition:** Recognizing when a high school girl gets her driver's license is an important rite of passage. With the attainment of a driver's license comes great responsibility. A quality key chain with a Bible verse or your girls' ministry logo and a Bible verse reference may be a special gift that a girl can look forward to receiving when she gets her driver's license. When bought in bulk, these items are very inexpensive and can be kept until each girl gets her license. Plan a special time to encourage each girl and remind her of the responsibility that having a drivers' license brings. This can be done in discipleship groups or in front of the whole youth group. Present the key ring, a short challenge in the responsibility and privilege of freedom, and pray a blessing of safety over her. This rite of passage could cause your girls to be more careful and think wisely enough to save their lives one day. This would be a time to encourage her to remain faithful to God and to her faith as she gains her new freedom. Many teen girls begin to "fade away" or drop out of youth activities when they earn the privilege of driving. You could use this time to challenge girls to remain faithful.

With the attainment of a driver's license comes great responsibility... This rite of passage could cause your girls to be more careful and think wisely enough to save their lives one day.

✿ **Progressive dinner for junior girls:** The purpose of this rite of passage is to promote unity and encourage leadership among the 11th grade girls in preparation to become role models and leaders for younger girls during their senior year of high school.

You will want to have this event sometime in the spring of their junior year before school is out for the summer. (Checking school and church calendars is vital to the success of this event. Sadly, most girls will choose prom and other events over a church event; therefore, wisely choose your date.) Each year we have chosen a Sunday night because it presents the least amount of conflicts and is in line with our discipleship meeting time.

To begin the dinner, meet at a specific time and place to travel together. It is usually a good policy to not permit teens to drive other teens, even if they have a driver's license and car. The liability is too great. Enlist youth workers or parents to drive. If your church is blessed to have a van or bus, riding together as a group will promote unity even more.

Choose three homes to each serve one portion of the meal. You may choose parents' or youth workers' homes, but I have found that older couples are perfect for this event. They love hosting the girls and always have great ways of showing their love and wisdom. This also provides an avenue to involve and connect the generations in your church.

Travel to the first home for appetizers. Estimate your travel times and let the hostess know when you will arrive. Since only a short time will be spent at each home, you will probably need to kindly move the girls on to the next home to stay on schedule. Travel to the second home for the main course and then to the third home for dessert.

I have found that older couples are perfect for this event. They love hosting the girls and always have great ways of showing their love and wisdom.

For the appetizers, you could suggest fruit and dip, cheese and crackers, and apple juice or punch. As a main course, you might want to try a mashed potato bar. For this, hosts would provide a big bowl of mashed potatoes with various toppings in smaller bowls such as cheese, chili, chopped chicken, chopped broccoli, onions, bacon, etc. Plastic parfait glasses will allow the girls to mingle and eat while they hold their dinner. You could also serve a sit-down dinner but will need to be careful of the time. For the dessert, you could suggest a chocolate fountain with fruit, marshmallows, pretzels, and other food items to cover with chocolate. Also consider serving cookies or other desserts.

At one of the homes, plan a short program to encourage the girls to prepare for strong leadership in their senior year. A meaningful gift is a votive candle for each girl. You can purchase candle wraps at craft stores and print each girl's name and a Bible verse on the wraps for the candles. (The information to purchase and print the votive wraps can be found on Web sites such as *www.uprint.com*.) Choose someone who is special to the girls to conduct the candle ceremony. Our student minister and his wife present the girls with their candle. They walk to each girl, light her candle, and say something personal, eye to eye, as they challenge each girl to let her light shine for Jesus Christ so she can influence younger girls in the youth group. This special gift will be a keepsake to remind them of their leadership responsibilities as rising senior girls. Some girls even take their candle to college and put it in their dorm rooms as a reminder of their responsibility to be a leader.

If you want to give a gift other than the candle, you may want to print Scripture cards to give each girl or even frame the verse as a gift. A good choice is Philippians 2:14-16, which says: "Do everything without grumbling and arguing, so that you may be blameless and pure, children of God who are faultless in a crooked and perverted generation, among whom you shine like stars in the world. Hold firmly the message of life. Then I can boast in the day of Christ that I didn't run in vain or labor for nothing." If the class has chosen a verse to live by, that would be a good choice as well.

Print colorful invitations to make the event seem special and important. Most invitation stores have sales on their printable invitations. Check with them and stock up when you find them. I recently purchased packages of really cute invitations for $1 per package. Normally they were $1 per invitation. I keep them for special events and offer the invitations to discipleship leaders for special events they do.

✿ **Decorate your dorm room:** This event is a rite of passage for senior girls. Plan this event close to their graduation from high school. The purpose is not only to give them great ideas for decorating their dorm room, but also to encourage them in making a decision to live for the Lord during the college years.

You could invite graduating senior girls and their mothers, their discipleship leaders, and/or Sunday School teachers for a sit-down dinner served buffet-style. Options for menus include:

- Chicken salad, pasta salad, croissants, chips, and dessert
- Lasagna, salad, bread, and dessert
- Sandwich trays, chips, and dessert
- Spaghetti, salad, bread, and dessert

Invite someone who is knowledgeable in interior decorating and college dorm decorating to come and demonstrate design ideas for the girls. Set up a display table with items and ideas. We developed a small booklet for the girls with the following topics:

Evaluating your space: Look at your space, then measure and decide what you can take. Talk to your roommate; decide who will bring the TV, microwave, and other big items. Most dorm rooms are not big enough for two of these items. Purchase bed extenders to add storage space under your bed.

Themes: Coordinate the color scheme with your roommate. (Or not!)

Tips for making your dorm room feel like home: Bring pillows, blankets, or a T-shirt quilt. Lamps and good lighting can also make a dorm room feel more homey.

Tips for decorating your dorm room to share your faith: Be careful what you put up on your walls. Think about how a non-Christian would view your room. When other girls know you are a Christian, they will watch what you do and say to see if you are living what you say you believe. Add pictures of friends in your discipleship group, mission trips, your parents and family, and framed Bible verses or your life verse. Leave your Bible out in an obvious place. Consider decorating with posters of your favorite Christian bands.

What to bring list: The following are items girls will possibly need for college:
   Bathroom: Find out if you have a community bath or private bath
   before buying some of these items:
• Towels and washcloths
• Bath mat
• Shower mat
• Hair dryer, curling iron, etc.
• Toothbrush holder
• Toilet paper
• Bathrobe
• Flip-flops for shower

- Shower curtain
- Extra hooks for towel and/or shelves to set over toilet
- Cotton swabs, cotton balls, etc. and small containers to hold them
- Shower basket to take back and forth for community baths or wire containers to hang on shower head in private bath

First aid kit: Store these items in a container and save yourself a trip to the student health center.
- Cough drops
- Bandages
- Hydrogen peroxide
- Rubbing alcohol
- Sunscreen
- Vitamins
- Allergy medicines
- Any prescriptions you need
- Nighttime and non-drowsy cold relief

Cleaning supplies: Disposable cleaning supplies are perfect for dorm living. Glass-cleaning and disinfectant wipes, as well as disposable toilet-cleaning sponges may save girls from spills and storage problems.
- Rubber gloves
- Toilet cleaner
- Glass cleaner
- Sink cleaner
- Air freshener
- Carpet deodorizer
- Hand soap and refill
- Dish cloths
- Dust pan
- Mop/broom and/or small vacuum
- Stain pre-treater
- Paper towels
- Dish-washing detergent
- Fabric freshener/wrinkle releaser
- One or two trash cans and trash bags
- Dusting spray and cloths
- Washing machine detergent and dryer sheets

School supplies: You may want to go to class before buying notebooks and books to see what your professor requires. Also, comparison shop before buying your school supples and textbooks. You will save a lot of money this way. You'll definitely need:

- Envelopes
- Stamps
- Stationery
- Stapler and staples
- Daily planner
- Tape
- Dividers
- Index cards
- Glue
- Push pins
- Spiral notebook
- Paper clips
- Notebook paper
- Computer paper
- Note pads/sticky notes
- Pens, highlighters, pencils
- Scissors
- Three-ring hole punch
- Three-ring binders
- Ink for printers
- Mounting tape for wall hangings

Miscellaneous supplies:
- Hammer and nails
- Bedding
- TV / DVD player
- Reading light
- Fan
- Flash light
- Large storage tubs
- Comfy chairs
- Alarm clock
- Full length mirror
- Phone
- Tissue
- Wall and/or desk calendar
- Water filter pitcher

- Blank CDs/jump drives
- Shelving paper for drawers
- Lock box for valuables
- Small blanket, quilt, or throw
- Tool kit
- Jumper cables for car
- Plates, cups, and eating utensils
- Over-the-door hooks
- Dry erase message board for your door
- Egg crate, foam pad, or feather mattress for bed
- Plastic bags and containers of all sizes
- Iron and ironing board (mini or over the door)
- Clothes hamper (with handles to take to laundry room)
- Quarters for laundry (some schools have laundry cards for purchase)
- Mini fridge (some schools provide these)
- Microwave (some schools provide these)

Mothers love the "what to bring list" and many take the booklet shopping and purchase what they need from the list. You can find lists for dorm room shopping on the Internet by researching the phrase "decorate your dorm room."

We asked our pastor's wife to speak at the event and present a challenge to the girls along with a small gift to put in their dorm room. One year she presented them with a small silver box tied with a pretty bow. The idea was to view their purity as a gift from God. They were to put the silver box in a central place in their dorm room to remind them who they are in Christ and that their gift of purity is a priceless treasure to be guarded until marriage. You could also attach a small Scripture card to the box by punching a hole in the card and stringing it onto the ribbon before you tie it on the box as a reminder of their purity.

Another year we presented each girl with a blessing ring. Blessing rings are decorative adornments for collecting your special cards, notes, and blessings. Some are silver rings with tons of ribbon and beads. Each time girls receive something special, such as a note of encouragement or a card, they can punch a hole in it and string it on their blessing rings. (To view a picture of a blessing ring, search for "blessing ring" using an online search engine.) We chose to use a picture of a girl graduate on ours and used ribbons and bows. The girls can display their graduation cards and special gifts in their dorm room as a reminder of the love people showed them during their graduation. They can go back and read the cards when they are feeling lonely or homesick.

A T-shirt quilt is also a great idea for keeping memories and making a girl's dorm room feel like home.

A T-shirt quilt is also a great idea for keeping memories and making a girl's dorm room feel like home. This will take some work from women in your church and the families of the senior girls. To do this, take some of a girl's T-shirts and cut out the main image. Then get someone who knows how to quilt to sew the shirt pieces together and add a quilt backing and binding. It is a wonderful memory for a girl to take to college to keep her warm and cozy while wrapped in memories of home.

We also purchased dorm room decorations and supplies from stores like Dollar Tree, Target, and Wal-Mart and showed the girls how to decorate their rooms with them. Then we gave away the items as door prizes at the end of the evening. This event makes a wonderful rite of passage for girls, and it is an evening they will remember for the rest of their lives. To top off the evening, we took pictures of every girl and her mother, framed them, and gave them to the girls.

✿ **Adopt a high school freshman:** Can you imagine what a freshman girl feels like the first day of high school? She walks onto the campus, has no idea where to go or where her classes are. But can you imagine how she would feel if a senior girl came by her house, picked her up for school, and showed her around campus, including where her classes meet? Pairing senior girls with freshmen girls for mentoring is a great way to help the freshman girl, but it also trains the senior girl for ministry and leadership. The senior girl could check on her adopted freshman on a weekly basis and see if she has questions, needs information, or simply just needs to talk about life. A text during the day just to say "I'm praying for you!" could make the younger girl's day. This is also a rite of passage for both the seniors and the freshmen since only senior girls would be allowed to adopt a freshman.

✿ **Mission trip superintendent:** Another area where seniors are used in leadership is on our annual mission trip. Ninth through twelfth graders are permitted to go on the mission trip, but only seniors are permitted to be the superintendents (or leaders) for the small groups. This entails a lot of responsibility on their part prior to and during the week of the mission trip. Each group has a group mom and dad, but the superintendent is really the leader. The adults are there to assist and guide. This rite of passage is one that senior students look forward to from the day they enter the student ministry.

✿ **Senior recognition day:** If your church does not celebrate high school graduation, it is important to make this an annual recognition not only for graduating senior girls, but also the senior boys. Each church may want to recognize their graduates in a different way, but here are some ideas:

- Allow graduates to wear their cap and gown on the Sunday morning before graduation, march into the worship service, and walk across the stage to shake hands with the pastor as he gives them a small gift for graduation.
- Purchase books or CDs for graduates.
- Host a graduate luncheon or dinner for senior students and their parents. A speaker who encourages the graduates, along with special music and a prayer time, is always meaningful.
- Plan a graduate breakfast on a Sunday morning for the graduates. They eat breakfast and enjoy Sunday School in someone's home or a nice restaurant to celebrate this milestone in their lives.
- Our seniors meet on Sunday night before graduation to affirm one another. This is a time when they can say affirming things to each other, reminisce about important times in the past, and say their good-byes before going away to college. This is always a special time since only seniors, their Sunday School teachers, and discipleship leaders are invited to this affirmation service. Many tears are shed and lots of hugs are given as they talk through this important season of their lives.

LEADERSHIP TRAINING

Don't ever underestimate the leadership abilities of senior high girls. Whenever possible, use senior high girls in leadership opportunities with middle school girls. It is amazing to see how they mature when given responsibility for younger students. They can lead devotions and help in small group discipleship for younger girls. (It is not wise to give senior high girls full responsibility for younger girls, so it is important to have adults monitoring as well, but it does cut down on the number of adults you need when senior high girls are involved.) This is great on-the-job training to develop girls as leaders.

You will always want to set guidelines for the senior high girls and give them the resources they need, but the average high school girl is very mature when given responsibility. Look for leadership training opportunities offered in your area for high school students.

BRIDGING THE GAP

Involving senior high girls in the overall life of the church is important. They need a place to belong when they come home from college or during Christmas break, spring break, or summer break. Being familiar with the church through worship and other events that are church-wide (such as volunteering to work in the nursery, helping out with food preparation, inviting some older, spiritually mature girls to attend women's conferences, etc.) will give them a feeling of belonging. When they come home from college, they will no longer feel like they belong in the student ministry. Helping students transition into the college or young adult ministry is important in keeping them involved in church after high school.

Mother-Daughter and Father-Daughter Events

MOST GIRLS WANT THE FAIRY TALE father-daughter relationship. However, when I think of the reality of most father-daughter relationships, I often think of the movie *Hope Floats*. In this movie, a little girl, Bernice, deals with the fact that her dad has asked her mother for a divorce. Bernice runs upstairs, packs her little suitcase, and runs back to the front door screaming, "I'm going with you, Daddy!" He replies that she can't go and that he needs to start a new life for himself, promising to come back and get her when he gets settled. She insists on going and throws her suitcase into the trunk of his car. He throws it out, gets into the car, and drives off. She runs behind the car screaming for her daddy to come back. It is a heartbreaking scene that rings all too true in real life.

God designed earthly fathers to provide a glimpse and a taste of our relationship with God. Unfortunately, most fathers do not recognize or understand the impact they have on their daughters' lives or own up to the responsibility they have in nurturing and loving them. Many fathers certainly do not understand the trauma suffered if they walk out the door for greener pastures.

In the beginning, God designed us with the fairy tale in mind (Eden), but because sin entered the world, that perfect world is unattainable here on earth. God still wants us to have great relationships, but often sin enters relationships and causes hurt, heartache, disappointment, and sometimes divorce. Whatever the situation is with the girls in your group, they need a healthy, loving relationship with their fathers.

A basic need for all girls is a strong, supportive, safe, and healthy family. Girls not only need a close and loving relationship with dad, but they need a meaningful relationship with mom as well. In fact, a mother is the number one influence in her daughter's life.[1] If a girl does not have the security of a strong family—a family in which the father is the protector, mom nurtures and cares for the family, and mom and dad love and respect each other—she will try to create a "family" in some other way. Sometimes a girl will try to create family with a boyfriend, intentionally get pregnant, join a gang, or even develop an inappropriate relationship with another female. Unhealthy Internet relationships involving sexual favors may be traded for words of love and affirmation from someone she doesn't even know in order to feel loved and accepted.

Sometimes fathers and daughters need to learn about each other even though they live under the same roof (or not). Because they often do not understand how to communicate clearly, they argue or ignore one another.

FATHER-DAUGHTER EVENTS

Often dads don't really know how to express love and concern to their daughters. When his daughter was a little girl, showing love was easier, but now she is maturing and growing into a young woman. Her father may feel awkward and at a loss for how to love and communicate with his daughter. Sometimes dads need an avenue for such communication and interaction with their daughters. Father-daughter events can open those doors.

Sometimes fathers and daughters need to learn about each other even though they live under the same roof (or not). Because they often do not understand how to communicate clearly, they argue or ignore one another. Parenting classes teaching fathers how to understand their daughters and father-daughter events are vitally important. A father-daughter event can give fathers and daughters ideas for communicating and understanding each other. These events can be fun and creative. You can choose to do a formal dress-up event or a less formal event that helps fathers and daughters interact.

When talking about father-daughter or mother-daughter events, I am often asked, "What if there are girls in my group who don't have one parent or the other?" Again, you have to know the girls in your group. Is there one girl who doesn't have a father or a mother or are there many girls who don't have a father or mother? The answer to this question will determine the event you plan (or if you plan a parent-daughter event at all).

If only one girl is missing either parent, then work individually with that girl to find someone who can escort her to the event, possibly a step-father, an uncle, a special person in her life, or even a brother. If many of the girls don't have fathers who are active in their lives, then you may want to forgo these events. Another idea that will lessen the sting of a mother-daughter or father-daughter event for a girl who doesn't have a mother or father is to call it "Mother, Daughter, Friend Shopping Trip" or "Father, Daughter, Friend Celebration."

In my church, we had one girl whose mother passed away a few years ago. We recently had a mother-daughter conference at our church, and she was not planning on attending. A few months before the event, a mother in our church, whose own teenage daughter had recently died of cancer, took the initiative and asked the girl to attend the conference with her. It was a blessing to each of them and helped them both in the healing process.

One of the girls in our group was adopted by a single mother, so she had a family friend volunteer to be a stand-in father for her and meet her at the event. We had another girl who had never known her father. She boldly asked one of our student ministers if he would escort her to the celebration. He gladly met her at the event, had his picture taken with her, sat with her, and prayed over her at the end. It turned out to be a special evening for both of them.

I would like to warn you against asking men in the church to pick up a girl from her house and bring her to the event. This is not a good idea. Avoiding situations like this will protect the man and your church from accusation and prevent putting the man and girl in an awkward situation. Having a family member drop off the girl at the event and asking the stand-in father to meet her there is the safest and best option.

Take some of the ideas below and modify them to fit the fathers and daughters in your church to create an avenue for interaction and communication to take place in healthy ways or to even improve good relationships.

❀ **THIRTY DAYS: TURNING THE HEARTS OF PARENTS AND TEENAGERS TOWARD EACH OTHER** (*LifeWay Press, 2003*): This is a parent-teen devotion to be completed together in thirty days. You may want to encourage dads to purchase this daily resource to use with their daughter one-on-one. There are thirty envelopes in this resource. You open an envelope each day and follow the instructions listed. It is a great way to open up communication where it has been closed or to improve an already good relationship.

✿ **Father-daughter celebration:** Girls love to dress up and look pretty, and deep down they love to spend time with their fathers. Capitalize on these two desires by celebrating the relationships between fathers and daughters. This can be a sit-down dinner, tea, or party. Involve fathers and daughters in the program—singing a duet, father-daughter program speakers, testimonies, skits, and so forth. Set up an area to make father-daughter pictures as the guests arrive. Invite someone to speak who understands father-daughter relationships or even a father-daughter team who can speak to the needs of fathers and daughters through their own personal testimonies. Top off the evening with each father reading a covenant to his daughter promising to live in a way that would protect his daughter's heart. He should sign the covenant in front of her. Encourage each father to put his arm around his daughter and pray a prayer of blessing over her. This can be a very touching time for fathers and daughters and may be the first time some fathers have ever prayed out loud for their daughters. Don't be afraid of embarrassing them. Deep down every father wants to pray for his daughter, but doesn't know how or thinks she might not be receptive. This is a good starting point.

Below is a covenant written by Rev. Tom Capps who spoke at our father-daughter celebration. You may want to provide frames for the girls to keep their covenant as a reminder of the special relationship with their dads.

(Daughter's name),

You are a precious gift from God.

He has entrusted you into my care and protection.

I love you, cherish you, and thank God for you.

I pledge to be the kind of man and father that

God wants me to be and you need me to be.

I will make mistakes because I am not perfect.

I will need your understanding and forgiveness.

I will provide for you, protect you, and pray for you,

not because it is my job, but because it is my joy

to be your father and to be involved in your life.

I promise to seek God's will and direction in my life

so I may be a faithful example of integrity and purity.

I promise to keep myself pure in mind and body.

Please take honor in yourself and hold tight to your gift of purity.
Follow the ways of God's truth. Continually guard your heart.
You ARE worth waiting for! You are precious and valuable to God,
and I pray that God will bless you and keep you in His will and in His hand.
May all your dreams come true.
With all my love and devotion,
(Dad's name)

✿ **Devotion book or talk sheets for fathers and daughters:** At the program just discussed, we gave every father and every daughter a devotion booklet. You can give the devotion booklet at any time, but it may be especially meaningful when given out at a father-daughter event or possibly for Father's Day. We enlisted people in our church to write devotions for fathers and daughters to use together. The devotions were the same for both the fathers and the daughters, but the life application was different for each of them. We called it "Twenty-One Days to your Daughter's Heart" and "Twenty-One Days to your Daddy's Heart." Fathers and daughters committed to read the devotions for 21 days and do what it said. Sometimes the father and daughter were directed to an interaction, and sometimes they did something separately. The idea is to think of Scripture or stories that would inspire fathers and daughters to communicate and love one another more. Coming from the fathers and daughters in your church, it will be more inspiring and will encourage dads to communicate more with each other on how to love their daughters. The following is an example of one of the devotions written by my daughter, Ginger:

DADDY'S HANDS

"My sheep hear my voice, I know them, and they follow me. I give them eternal life, and they will never perish—ever! No one will snatch them out of My hand." —John 10:27-28

My favorite thing about my daddy is the comfort I find in him, but my favorite physical trait is his hands. His hands could never be used to model in magazines or TV commercials because he bites his fingernails and sometimes his skin is cracked and dry. Nevertheless, they are big, strong hands, and I think they are beautiful!

These are the hands that tossed me in the air and caught me as I giggled and laughed as a 2-year-old. Those same hands held me when I was scared of moving to a new place. They spanked my bottom when I willfully disobeyed and put myself in danger, and they thumped the back of my head when I acted up in church. As I grew up, those hands gave me a high five when I made the honor roll my senior year of high school, and then a few months later moved me into my college dorm room. Those hands signed for my first car, and patted me on the back when I graduated from college.

I felt incredible strength as those hands held my arm as I walked down the aisle on my wedding day. Then only a few years later those big, rough hands so tenderly held my baby daughter as she was dedicated to the Lord on Easter Sunday morning. A year later those same hands wiped tears from my eyes, and then his, when we didn't know if my premature twin boys were going to live. Even though I am 30 years old now, just last Sunday he held my hand during church as if to say, "Ginger, I'm still your daddy, and I will do anything to protect you."

As I think of my earthly daddy's hands, it brings a smile to my face remembering all the things he has done for me. He has made many sacrifices for me throughout my life which I am extremely thankful for. I know that my daddy would give his life for me because he loves me so much. I don't think he would do that for just anyone!

Somehow when I look at my Daddy's hands, it reminds me of God. As I think of my Heavenly Father's hands, it overwhelms me knowing all that He has done for me. To think of the pain He suffered so I may live eternally in heaven is amazing! As much as my Daddy loves me, nothing compares to my Heavenly Father's sacrifice on the cross. What Jesus did for me is the most incredible love I have ever known.

Have you held your daughter's hand recently? Find an opportunity to hold her hand in a way to let her know you love her and want to protect her. This may not be the coolest thing to do, but she will appreciate the effort you are making to say, "I love you" and "I am here for you" in a different way.

Prayer: Heavenly Father, thank you for my daughter. Please protect her today as only You can. Protect her mentally, physically, emotionally, and spiritually. I pray that I can be the daddy that she needs as she becomes a woman. Give me the courage to hold her hand to show her how much I love her on a daily basis so she will realize how much You love her as well. In Jesus' name, Amen.

The devotion for the daughter is the same except for the ending:
Have you held your daddy's hand recently? Find an opportunity to hold his hand. This may not be the coolest thing for you to do, but do it to let him know how special he is to you. Look at your dad's hands. Think about all of the things he has done for you and the sacrifices he has made so that you have what you need. Write him a note and tell him

how much you appreciate all that he has done for you.

Prayer: *Heavenly Father, thank You for my Daddy. Thank you for the sacrifices he has made for me and our family. Help me to show him daily how much I love him. Protect him today in all he does. Thank You for Your amazing love and for the sacrifice You made for me on the cross. In Jesus' name I pray, Amen.*

You will be surprised at the devotions the fathers and daughters in your church will create. You can print the devotions yourself and staple them together in a small booklet or have it printed at a local printing company. As an option, it may be more suitable for your church to create talk sheets for fathers and daughters to use together.

✿ **Father-daughter sporting events:** Other events you can plan for the fathers and daughters could be a father-daughter sporting event such as a softball game, volleyball game, basketball, or flag football event. Fathers and daughters on the same team competing against other fathers and daughters would make it incredibly fun. You may even want to invite families to watch. We will talk more about sporting events for girls in the next chapter.

MOTHER-DAUGHTER EVENTS

Below you will find some ideas regarding mother-daughter events. Take these ideas and adapt them to fit the mothers and daughters in your group:

✿ **Mother-daughter conference:** A mother-daughter conference is a great way to give moms and daughters a comfortable place in which to interact with each other. Doing fun activities together, learning about each other, and having activities that promote good conversation are all ways to enhance or even repair mother-daughter relationships.

If your church is smaller and you cannot afford to have a mother/daughter conference at your church, you might want to attend an event sponsored by someone else. LifeWay sponsors "You and Your Girl" conferences across the United States each year. This conference features Vicki Courtney and others who bring eye-opening messages covering mother-daughter dynamics from a biblical perspective, including: what every girl wants her mom to know, things moms want to tell their daughters, and talking about your personal faith with your daughter in relevant terms.

For more information, you can go online to *www.lifeway.com/women* to find out where the You and Your Girl conferences will be held. This is definitely an economical option for your church if the location is close to your area.

If there is not a You and Your Girl conference coming close to you, consider partnering with several other churches to pull together an event for moms and daughters. At one mother-daughter conference, each mother and daughter presented each other a piece of jewelry as a significant reminder of their love for one another. It was a necklace with the words "I am here for you!" engraved on the heart-shaped charm.

Doing fun activities together, learning about each other, and having activities that promote good conversation are all ways to enhance or even repair mother-daughter relationships.

✿ **Mother-daughter tea:** Little girls love to have a tea party with their dolls, stuffed animals, and imaginary friends. Teenage girls like to dress up and have a tea party too! You may want to have this event at someone's house or even a tea room. Special invitations, tea cakes, tiny desserts, scones, and different kinds of flavored tea are all a part of making this event special. You may want to have an interactive time between the moms and daughters or have someone give a short motivational talk to them. An inexpensive gift, such as matching teacups, for each mother and daughter to remember the day is also a nice gesture.

Choosing a theme for your tea party is a good idea, and you could even have a special verse. "If Teacups Could Talk" is a possible theme for your tea event. If teacups had ears, just think about all the important conversations, advice, and wisdom they have heard through the years between mothers and daughters. If they could talk, what are the important things they would tell us? This is a cute way to pass on important wisdom from mothers to daughters and even vice versa. Another possible idea is to teach girls (and mothers) tea etiquette during the event.

✿ **Mother-daughter shopping trip:** A shopping trip for moms and daughters can be risky unless you know the mothers and daughters have pretty good relationships already. Sometimes shopping can be a stressful time, especially if the daughter wants to purchase items of which the mother doesn't approve. We've had pretty successful mother-daughter shopping trips so far. One was an overnight trip to Atlanta. We ate in a nice restaurant, stayed in a hotel, and went Christmas shopping the next day. The moms carried snacks and all the girls and moms gathered in one room for a pajama party. Even though two mothers and two daughters stayed in each hotel room, it turned out to be an expensive trip. The next time, we planned a one-day trip leaving early on a Saturday morning and returning that afternoon. Again, you have to know the moms and daughters in your church. Some of the girls wanted to shop at an upscale mall while others wanted to shop at a discount mall. You can plan a back-to-school shopping trip, a Christmas shopping trip, or even a shopping trip to see who can purchase the best outfit for the least amount of money. More often than not, girls want their moms along since they usually control the purse strings. If you have a church van or bus, it is always fun to ride together. The fellowship on the trip is part of the fun. Daughters love seeing their moms relax and have fun with other moms.

FAMILY MISSION TRIPS OR PROJECTS

Providing avenues for girls to go on a mission trip with their mom or dad (or both) is an excellent way to help girls learn how to work together and grow closer in their relationships with parents. For many years, churches have provided mission trips for teens only. Girls come home having experienced a life-changing trip, but moms and dads have not had that same advantage. It is wonderful when both can experience the same life-changing adventure. More and more churches are planning family mission trips so that families can learn the dynamics of working and ministering together. Planning a mission trip (either foreign or local) for families can be an avenue to connect girls to their families and the entire church family. Local mission projects are less expensive, and you can line up projects such as fathers and daughters working in a soup kitchen or homeless shelter together, or mothers and daughters sorting clothes in a Salvation Army store. The ideas can be endless when you begin to think and plan for mission projects.

DOING A GOOD THING

Most parents want to be involved in their teenage daughter's lives, but many don't know how. Girls need their fathers but often sabotage their relationships unknowingly. Fostering mother-daughter and father-daughter relationships is an important area of girls' ministry and can make a great difference in families and the future of teenage girls. The following story has forever changed the way I view parent ministry.

In November of 2006, I was headed to Nashville, Tennessee, to teach a girls' ministry class at the National Women's Ministry Forum. As I was sitting in the airport waiting on my connection, I noticed a very well-dressed gentleman watching me. It was obvious that he was a well-to-do businessman, but every time I looked up, he was looking at me and didn't turn away. It was a very uncomfortable situation, so I was happy when they called me to board the plane. I found my seat and was getting settled in when I looked up and—you guessed it—saw the same man take the seat next to mine. He was my seat mate on a 250-passenger plane! He began to ask questions about where I was going and why. When I told him I was teaching a class on girls ministry, he became very interested and asked one question after another. I was focused on what I planned to teach that day and was not really interested in talking, but I briefly told him that I teach teenage girls in church how to love the Lord with all of their hearts, how to accept Him into their lives, and how to make wise decisions based on the Bible so they will have the best life possible. I also added that I teach parents how to love their daughters so they will look back on life with no regrets. He was quiet for the rest of the flight, but as we began to prepare for landing, he pulled a gold necklace out of his shirt collar and handed it to me. The military tag-style necklace held the picture of a beautiful blonde girl wearing a crown. For a moment I was speechless, but then realized there was more to the story. As I looked at the necklace in my hand, I asked him to tell me about the girl. With tears in his eyes, he turned the necklace over and engraved on the back was the birth date and death date of his precious daughter, Kelsey. He said:

"Kelsey was a wonderful daughter. She was captain of a national championship cheerleading squad at her school, homecoming queen, and a camp counselor at Sharp Top Cove, a camp for Young Life students. She played basketball for her church and loved people, especially her family.

In February of this year, she was traveling to meet her mother and me at a basketball game. It had been raining, and she ran off the road and flipped her car. She was killed instantly. There were over 3,000 people at her funeral. We loved our daughter very much, and our hearts are deeply grieved at her being taken so young. Two weeks after the funeral, the toxicology report came back. Kelsey's blood alcohol level was three times the legal limit, and there were traces of cocaine in her blood. We were shocked and devastated. We never dreamed anything like that was going on in her life."

He then turned and looked at me with a renewed strength and confidence as he continued in a slow, very calculated way. "You are doing a good thing. Don't give up. What you are doing is important. When you get to your conference, it is important for you to tell those women about my daughter. Tell them to continue teaching girls to make wise decisions. Tell them to continue teaching parents how to love and be involved in their daughters' lives so they will not have the regret this dad has."

You are doing a good thing. Don't give up! Continue teaching moms and dads how to love their daughters and how to be involved in their lives. What you are doing is important work with an eternal impact in the kingdom of God.

When I look back and remember that man staring at me in the airport, I know my meeting him and sitting next to him was orchestrated by God. When he told me the story of his daughter and encouraged me to continue my work with teenage girls and their parents, I know it was of God. I tell this man's story every opportunity I have to encourage women to understand the importance of parents being involved in their daughter's lives.

And now I say to you: You are doing a good thing. Don't give up! Continue teaching teenage girls how to make wise decisions and to love Jesus with all their hearts. Continue teaching moms and dads how to love their daughters and how to be involved in their lives. What you are doing is important work with an eternal impact in the kingdom of God.

1. Nicole Whitacre, "Mom: The Primary Influence in a Girl's Life," Crosswalk.com [online], cited 26 February 2009. Available from the Internet: *http://www.crosswalk.com/1356743/page1/*.

CHAPTER 11

Physical Health for Girls

*I*F YOU SPEND MUCH TIME WITH TEEN GIRLS, you will notice that many girls do not eat healthy foods, exercise regularly, or get proper rest. Often girls are overweight or too thin because of poor habits on both ends of the physical health spectrum. Many girls sit at their computers when not in school and get very little exercise during the week. Physical education programs have been cut from many schools, and a girl's participation in sports or physical activity declines significantly as she gets older. By the time she is 16 or 17, only 1 in 7 attends P.E. class daily, and 15-30 percent report no regular physical activity at all.[1] Fast food restaurants are on every street corner, and with fast-moving lifestyles, girls often eat on the run, filling up with empty calories.

What can we do in girls' ministry to promote healthier lifestyles and enable girls to live longer and more productive lives for Jesus Christ? Not only is teaching and modeling health important, but it is also our responsibility. The Bible speaks about honoring our bodies as the temple of the Holy Spirit. If a girl's body is not physically fit, she will not be productive as a Christian young woman. If she is not getting enough sleep or exercise (or is exercising too much), she will not have the energy to minister to others. If a girl is overweight, she may be adding extra stress to her heart and joints, which could have long-term effects. Being healthy is an important part of being a Christian.

Eating disorders continue to be prevalent in our society today. With the media's obsession with outward appearance, it's no wonder that such a mentality has filtered down into girls' (and women's) everyday lives, setting up a standard and creating an expectation that is physically and emotionally damaging. Girls in your ministry will fall somewhere along the spectrum—from overly thin to grossly obese. Your goal should be to teach all of the girls how to live healthy lifestyles and take care of their bodies so they can be more effective for Christ. The following statistics on eating disorders can be found on Students Against Destructive Decisions' Web site:[2]

- Nationwide, 12.3 percent of high school students had gone without eating for 24 hours or more to lose weight or to keep from gaining weight during the last 30 days. (2005 CDC Youth Risk Behavior Surveillance)
- During the last 30 days, 6.3 percent of students nationwide had taken diet pills, powders, or liquids without a doctor's advice to lose weight or to keep from gaining weight. (2005 CDC Youth Risk Behavior Surveillance)
- Nationwide, 4.5 percent of students had vomited or taken laxatives to lose weight or to keep from gaining weight during the last 30 days. Overall the prevalence of having vomited or taken laxatives to lose weight or to keep from gaining weight was higher among female (6.2 percent) than male (2.8 percent) students. (2005 CDC Youth Risk Behavior Surveillance)
- Approximately 1-2 percent of late adolescent or adult women suffer from bulimia. (Academy for Eating Disorders)
- One percent of female adolescents suffer from anorexia. In other words, 1 out of every 100 young women between 10-20 years old is starving herself, sometimes to death.
- Four percent, or 4 out of 100, of college-age women have bulimia.

On the other end of the spectrum:

- About 31 percent of American teenage girls and 28 percent of boys are somewhat overweight.
- An additional 15 percent of American teen girls and nearly 14 percent of teen boys are obese.

In addition to these statistics, similar facts bear out the prevalence of girls' struggles with weight and body image:

- Thirty-five percent of girls 6 to 12 years of age have been on at least one diet.[3]
- Sixty-nine percent of girls wish they were thinner.[4]

- Sixty-three percent of girls think about improving their body in some way every single day.[5]
- While 19% of teenagers are overweight, 67% think they need to lose weight.[6]

Eating disorders and disordered eating are a serious physical and psychological disorder not to be taken lightly. It is important to refer girls whom you suspect have an eating disorder for professional treatment. Do research to find doctors and psychologists in your local area who specialize in treating eating disorders. This could mean the difference between life and death for the girls affected.

Even if your girls do not suffer from an eating disorder, chances are strong that some of them struggle with disordered eating. This term refers to troublesome or unhealthy eating behaviors, such as restrictive dieting, bingeing, or purging, which occur less frequently or are less severe than those required to meet the full criteria for the diagnosis of an eating disorder. This type of eating can refer to changes in eating patterns in relation to an event, illness, appearance, or to prepare for an athletic event. (How many of your girls go on a diet to fit into that certain dress for prom? How many of your moms go on a diet to lose weight before going on vacation?) It is an unhealthy relationship with food in which food becomes an enemy rather than merely a means by which to fuel the body.

How do we teach girls to take care of their bodies? Often, we think sitting in a classroom and teaching the Bible is the only responsibility of the church, but I believe teaching girls about every area of their lives—spiritual, emotional, physical, mental, and social—is important in their effectiveness for Christ.

Eating disorders and disordered eating are a serious physical and psychological disorder not to be taken lightly.

HEALTH-FOCUSED EVENTS FOR GIRLS

The following events and education ideas will help you get started in teaching girls to take care of their bodies.

✿ **Exercise class for teen girls:** Offering an exercise class for girls in your church can be a fun event that encourages girls to develop a healthy lifestyle and take care of their bodies. If their friends are involved, if it's fun, and if they're comfortable, girls will want to be involved. Recruit a woman trained in leading exercise programs to teach the class, which should be held in a place where the girls don't feel like people are watching them.

There are many different methods you can use for exercise: kickboxing, aerobics, pilates, karate, and more. Using current Christian music as your background music will also expose girls to healthy music styles. You may want to meet two or three times a week at a time that is convenient for the girls and leader. You may choose to have a short devotion related to taking care of your body before you begin. Some of the topics to include are good nutrition, getting enough rest, ways to get exercise naturally during the day, and prayer. Prayer and meditating on Scripture helps relax your mind and body and will help you feel better throughout the day.

✿ **Powder puff football:** This event has been one of the most popular events for teen girls in our church. When I first joined the staff as the director of girls ministry, I was talking with some of the high school girls and asked what kind of girls' ministry events they would like to do. Immediately our pastor's daughter yelled, "Powder puff football!" I'll have to admit I was a little skeptical and had to think about how we could incorporate that into our church programming. The Lord touched my heart, and I realized this would not only be a fun event, but it would also teach the girls how to work together as a team, how to be good sports, and would get them up and moving.

Powder puff has also became an outreach event for the community. We had several hundred people come out to watch the first year. We advertised well, and it was the biggest thing going on in our city that day. During the event, we always have someone present the gospel, and the first year, a father of one of the players raised his hand to accept Christ. During practice, the coaches always do a devotion with the girls, encouraging them to run the race to the best of their ability and to always keep in mind loving others and working as a team. We open the teams to girls in our church and community. Girls can invite their unsaved friends to play, and often we have girls who accept Christ and join our church because of this event. Below you will find some of the logistics for the event:

Guidelines for coaches

- There will be one head coach (usually male—they know more about football!) and one assistant coach per team (usually female)
- Each coach will recruit student assistant coaches.
- Coaches will draw their team randomly at the organizational meeting. Each coach will review the rosters to make sure the teams are divided evenly. Each coach will have the opportunity to meet their teams briefly at the end of the meeting.
- There will be two scheduled practices. Coaches are asked not to practice at other times and locations with their teams for liability reasons.
- Each coach should stress team spirit and having Christlike attitudes to the girls. Please remember that winning is not the important thing.
- Each coach is asked to do a devotion and have prayer before practices.

Awards

- There will be a Most Christlike Award for each team. This is the most important award for the game. (These certificates are made on the computer and framed.)
- Trophies and awards will be given the Wednesday after the game. Teams are asked to attend the youth meeting and sit together. (The "trophy" is a plaque, purchased at a local trophy store for around $25, with a picture of the winning team on it. These trophies are added each year to a wall in the student area.)

Uniforms

- Every girl must wear a T-shirt in her team color. (T-shirts may be donated by area businesses. It is important to have numbers on the back. Another alternative is to buy plain white T-shirts and let the girls decorate their shirts with fabric pens in their team color.)
- Long basketball shorts with a drawstring or long pants with a drawstring are required during the games (to prevent pants from being pulled down with the flag). Inappropriate clothing will result in disqualification.

• Every girl is required to purchase a mouthpiece which must be worn at all times when playing. (This is to prevent knocking out your pearly whites!)

Other

• Encourage parents to come and bring their picnic lunch and lawn chairs.
• Consider selling drinks and candy.
• Permission forms must be signed and handed in before practice.

Powder puff rules

The following rules have been adapted for Powder Puff from Upward Unlimited™. The game will be played with eight players on offense and eight players on defense.

Offense Rules:

• Each team will consist of two down lineman and six skill players. Skill players may be in any formation.
• The offense is given four downs to advance 10 yards for a first down.
• Each team can run or pass.
• All false starts will result in 5 yard loss.
• Lining up offsides is a "no-call."
• Coaches will not be allowed on the field except during time outs.
• Each team will have two 3-minute time outs per half.
• There will be punts and kick offs, but no rush on the punts or returns. On-side kicks are allowed. The ball is to be fair caught or downed.
• The extra point may be for one point or two. If for one point, only passing is allowed from 5 yard line. If for two points, you can run or pass, but from the 10 yard line.
• There will be a 45-second play clock to hurry play.
• There will be two 20-minute halves.
• Fumbles are not live except for the snap to the quarterback.
• Blocks are legal from anywhere on the field. No blocks in the back.
• Blocks are permitted above the waist only.
• The clock will be continuously running except to set the chains and inside of two minutes if a player goes out of bounds.
• Flag guarding, holding, and stiff arming will be monitored with warnings, and can result in a 5-yard penalty.

Defense:

- Each team will consist of two rushing linemen and six skill defensive backs.
- No blitzes allowed. Only the two down linemen may rush.
- Defensive pass interference results in 15-yard penalty or automatic first down.
- Coaches will not be allowed on the field except during time outs.
- Other defenders can pass the line of scrimmage on a run play.
- Tackling and off sides will be monitored with warnings.
- Illegal rushes will earn a 15-yard penalty.
- Final decisions, when needed, will be made by the lead official.

Powder puff football for junior high and senior high girls is an opportunity to involve many people in your church. Of course you can adapt these positions to your church and community. Some of the possible positions to fill for the game are:

- Head coaches (usually male)
- Assistant coaches (usually female)
- Nurse
- Trainer
- Water boy or girl
- Lunch servers
- Photographer
- Ball boys or girls (great for the younger children)
- Student coaches (high school guys in your church)
- Someone to present the plan of salvation. This can be a male or female but needs to be someone who is respected and has influence in the community. You could enlist a "celebrity" athlete in your area who lives an exemplary Christian lifestyle.
- Chain gang: girls who don't really want to play but still want to be involved
- Referees: You will want referees who know the rules and are experienced in refereeing.
- Cheerleaders: Occasionally we have some guys who will think it's fun to dress up and cheer. Sometimes the guys would rather help coach. We are flexible on this, and if we don't have cheerleaders, it is no big deal.

We also ask businesses to sponsor the event. We put their name on the program. Some businesses may donate the team T-shirts, food, printing the programs (if you choose to have a program), or even the plastic flags.

As you can see, this event can be as big as you would like to make it, or you may choose just to meet at a park on a Saturday afternoon, divide the girls up, and play flag football. It is entirely up to you. Whatever you decide, always make sure that you draw a spiritual application from the game—teamwork, good sportsmanship, and healthy bodies.

✿ **Team Sports:** Girls often will sit on the sidelines talking while boys are playing sports. I've come to realize that many girls don't care to play competitive sports with boys, but they will play sports with other girls. Organized team sports for girls are more popular than you would think. Many girls love basketball, volleyball, softball, tennis, and even golf. Organizing teams or leagues for teenage girls is an important part of girls' ministry. If you are part of a larger church, talk with your recreation minister about organizing teams for teenage girls.

✿ **Women in Sport™ conference:** A friend of mine is on staff with Fellowship of Christian Athletes, and her job is to focus on female coaches and athletes. In planning to meet the needs of the female athletes, she planned the Women in Sport™ Conference, complete with a speaker and breakout sessions for the girls and coaches. She built relationships with coaches and asked them to bring their teams. We hosted the conference at our church, and it turned out to be a wonderful event for several hundred female coaches and athletes. Many girls accepted Christ as their Savior, and many of the female coaches are attending a Bible study especially for them. It has become an annual event, and the girls really look forward to the conference. You can find out more information about organizing a Women in Sport™ conference or beginning a ministry to female coaches and athletes in your area by contacting Kaye O'Sullivan at *kosullivan@fca.org*. This is an untapped area of girls' ministry in most areas, but many coaches and athletes are open to this type of ministry.

✿ **Cooking Class:** Many girls do not know how to cook. You can offer a cooking class that teaches them not only how to cook, but also how to prepare healthy meals. You can enlist a nutritionist in your church to teach the class or to co-teach the class with a woman who loves to cook. Girls can try out recipes, do research on recipes they'd like to try, and work together to find healthy alternatives to foods they like.

In addition to offering these classes and sporting events, you can model the behavior you want girls to adopt by offering healthy choices at events. In addition to the traditional snacks (chips, dip, cookies, etc.), also provide fruits, nuts, popcorn, and other healthy options. When planning an event that requires a menu, think of ways to provide healthier alternatives if possible (a sub sandwich-building contest instead of a marshmallow-eating contest). The goal is not for girls to feel guilty because they don't "measure up" in some way, but rather to help them become smarter in making choices. Planning events and educating girls on how to develop a healthy lifestyle will give them tools to help them become more effective for the Kingdom.

1. "GoGirlGo!," Women's Sports Foundation [online], cited 26 February 2009. Available from the Internet: http://www.womenssportsfoundation.org/GoGirlGo.aspx.

2. "Statistics: Eating Disorders," SADD [online], cited 26 February 2009. Available from the Internet: http://www.sadd.org/stats.htm#eatingdisorders.

3. Adam R. Holz, "Is Average the New Ugly?," Plugg'd In (August 2007), 4.

4. ElleGirl (February 2006).

5. "CosmoGirl Body Image Survey," CosmoGirl (February 2006).

6. "Girl Stats + Studies—Factoids: Girl Statistics and Studies," Respect RX [online], cited 26 February 2009. Available from the Internet: http://www.respectrx.com/archives/girl_stats_studies/.

CHAPTER 12

Planning and Organization

$\mathcal{E}$ VERY CHURCH HAS A UNIQUE ministry personality, and every minister has a unique personal leadership style. But every minister must learn to be organized, or he or she will not be completely effective in leading the ministry that God has entrusted to him or her. Not everyone who is in a leadership position in the church has the spiritual gift of administration, but every leader can learn to organize and plan ministry events effectively. Some people think planning and organization are boring, unnecessary, and stifling to creativity, but those people will soon find that other church staff, parents, and even girls become frustrated and maybe even critical when girls' ministry events are unorganized and chaotic. Most parents want to know details about the events in which their daughters are involved because they want to know the girls are safe and protected.

Sometimes young women who are drawn to girls' ministry think this ministry simply means hanging out with the girls, hosting fun events, being on stage in front of groups of girls, and helping girls with problems they face. But they fail to realize that girls' ministry takes organization, planning, and a lot of hard work behind the scenes. A "fly by the seat of your pants" mind-set will catch up with you sooner or later.

One of the top mistakes in girls' ministry is trying to do everything alone instead of taking the time and energy to build a leadership team. Even in a smaller church, the person in charge of girls' ministry must have others who come alongside and help organize, plan, and implement an effective ministry. Not doing so will result in burn-out.

In this section, I will discuss several ways to organize and plan for girls' events and ministry. If you follow these basic guidelines to help you become organized and plan effectively for ministry to teenage girls, parents will feel comfortable allowing their daughters to be involved, girls will know what to expect, and there will be less confusion, allowing the Holy Spirit to work in the lives and hearts of those involved. We will discuss these guidelines with the assumption that you already have an established girls' ministry in your church and that your pastor and other staff are on board and supportive of ministry to teenage girls.

PLANNING TIPS

Before you begin to plan different events for teenage girls, there are some basic organizational tips that will help you to successfully plan for a comprehensive ministry to teenage girls in your church:

✿ **Keep an organized, up-to-date calendar of church events, personal appointments, and girls' ministry events.** Many people choose to keep a calendar in their phone or laptop. This is fine in the modern world of technology, but being able to view the entire month is important. Make sure you see the big picture to determine if you are overloaded with personal appointments or if you are overloading the girls with events. Looking at the big picture will enable you to spread out the events so you will not have a bunch of events cluttered into one weekend, whether they are girls' ministry events or not. It is important to look at the church-wide schedule, including the student ministry and women's ministry schedules, as well as school calendars to make sure you are not planning an event on top of something else already happening. Spreading out events across several months is a wise financial choice as well.

Not everyone who is in a leadership position in the church has the spiritual gift of administration, but every leader can learn to organize and plan ministry events effectively.

✿ **Block out time in your schedule for planning.** If you are the girls' minister or director of the girls' ministry in your church, whether paid or a volunteer, it is important for you to take the time to sit quietly before God and ask Him for a vision for the girls' ministry. After you have taken the time to really listen and hear what God is saying to you, put your vision on paper and share this with the minister to whom you are responsible (either the student minister, women's minister, or the pastor). I work on the student ministry staff and answer directly to the student minister of our church. I share the vision and ideas for ministry with him twice a year to make sure I am on track according to our ministry plans and budget. He either gives me the go ahead for events or we talk through alternate plans. This also provides accountability.

✿ **After you have approval from the minister in charge of your area, gather a planning team.** Think about the event and what it will take to organize it. Keep in mind that well-planned large events require at least six months to a year of planning.

Girls' ministry takes organization, planning, and a lot of hard work behind the scenes. A "fly by the seat of your pants" mind-set will catch up with you sooner or later.

✿ **Pray about those who have the talents and abilities needed to accomplish this task.** You will meet ahead of time with the entire team at least once, depending on the extent of planning needed for the event. Training and empowerment is essential when working with teams of volunteers. You don't want to insult their intelligence, but often volunteers are willing to help you realize your vision for the event but don't know what to do or how to do it. Giving volunteers the necessary training and resources will enable them to be successful and will help the event run more smoothly. After the event is over, it is vital to recognize and thank the team for their hard work.

✿ **Keep a task list and organizational notebook for each event.** You will want to add a time line for tasks to be finished and who is responsible for completing them. Assign specific tasks to specific people and then empower them to do the job. Keep in touch with them and assist them if necessary, but allow them to have ownership. Don't micromanage.

✿ **Communicate with team members regularly, letting them know important information about the event.** This will help the event run more smoothly. If someone has to look for you the day of the event to find out the answer to a dozen questions, you have not done your job well. Giving others pertinent information does not make you less important; it causes you to appear confident and efficient. Sometimes there are last minute questions that only you can answer, but these should be minimal.

✿ **Keep your plans for an event in a computer file and in an organizational notebook.** Keeping information in a computer file is easy and convenient, but printing off the documents and keeping them in a notebook is handy as well because everything is together. On the day of the event or trip, pick up the notebook, and you'll have everything you need. You may want to organize a notebook for each of the team members so they will have everything they need as well. You can include registration forms, permission forms, and even evaluation forms for the end of the event. Having a hard copy of everything also gives you a back-up in case your computer crashes.

Keep good records in a notebook. This will be a great reference point if you repeat the event next year or some time in the future. If you have planned well, involved a team, and empowered others to do their job, you will host a well-run event that will help you accomplish your vision and purpose.

✿ **After the event, shred permission forms** since they may contain private information that could fall into the wrong hands.

Involving teen girls, college students, and young women in the planning process will ensure that you are not just planning events that feel comfortable to you.

✿ **Involve teen girls or young adult/college girls in planning.** One of the biggest mistakes made in girls' ministry is trying to copy women's ministry events for teen girls. That's like trying to fit a square peg into a round hole. Involving teen girls, college students, and young women in the planning process will ensure that you are not just planning events that feel comfortable to you. Remember, you are at a different stage of life, and what appeals to you probably won't appeal to a teenage girl.

✿ **Communicate information to girls often and clearly.** You can plan a perfect event, but if you do not communicate details to the girls and their parents, you will not have a well-attended event. In the first chapter, we addressed communication with iGeneration girls. Below are some important tips on communicating information when planning for girls' ministry and events.

1. Communicating details to girls through Facebook, text messages, videos, and other modern ways is important. Parents, on the other hand, may need forms of communication like a newsletter or postcard in the mail with details on upcoming events.

2. Quarterly parent meetings are a good way to keep parents informed of upcoming events and give them opportunities to ask questions. You can also use this time as a training of sorts. You could help keep parents informed about issues that teen girls face, challenge them to be the spiritual leaders of their daughters, and encourage them in their own walk with Christ.

3. Prepare a flier, brochure, or other form of communication to distribute at least twice a year. Include upcoming events with details about cost, sign-up deadlines, and other pertinent information. Keep this information available in the student area and other places in your church. This will inform not only parents and their daughters, but the church body as well. You may find new volunteers for girls ministry as they approach you about becoming involved in an activity that interests them.

4. Before trips, host a parent meeting to go over details of the trip. Discuss important information about the trip, and allow parents to turn in permission forms, pay registration fees, and ask questions. You can also use this time to pray for the upcoming event.

Determine your strengths and weaknesses and do what only you can do. Surround yourself with women and girls who have strengths that are your weakness.

✿ **Give away your ministry.** Determine your strengths and weaknesses and do what only you can do. Surround yourself with women and girls who have strengths that are your weakness. Anything that a volunteer woman, college girl, or teenage girl can do, give it away! Recruit, train, and empower volunteers to plan and implement girls' ministry.

WHEN THINGS GO WRONG

Sometimes unexpected things happen. When they do, allow God to work His plan. Don't fret. Just step back and ask the Lord what He would have you do. One weekend conference at our church was totally interrupted by a fast-moving ice storm in Atlanta. We had planned a Friday night through Saturday morning conference. We invited a girls' band from Chattanooga, Tennessee, to lead the praise and worship, and the speaker was driving in from Columbia, South Carolina. The morning of the conference, the weather forecast called for an ice storm beginning Friday evening and lasting until mid-morning on Saturday. I panicked for a moment but soon realized that only God can cause an ice storm. I took quick action, calling all the girls to tell them to bring their sleeping bags and plan to sleep in the church. The speaker made it, but the band was stranded in Tennessee. I called four well-respected teenage boys from our youth group to help. They wore wigs and imitated the band to make the announcement that the band would not be there. The girls thought it was funny. The boys went home, but we still had praise and worship music—from a CD. It turned out to be a wonderful weekend.

Sometimes unexpected things happen. When they do, allow God to work His plan.

Just a word of wisdom: when planning events, it is a good idea to have a backup plan just in case the weather doesn't cooperate. When unexpected things occur, remember that God is in control, especially when circumstances are totally out of your hands. What you think is a disaster in the making may be orchestrated by God.

IN CLOSING

I pray God's richest blessings on your ministry. I am praying for each woman who will read this book. Again, I want to remind you that you are doing a good thing. Don't give up! Continue teaching girls how to make wise decisions and to love Jesus with all their hearts. Continue teaching moms and dads how to love their daughters and be involved in their lives. What you are doing is important work with an eternal impact on the kingdom of God.

Girls' Ministry in the Smaller Church

Thirty years ago, my husband accepted the call to be the student minister at a very small church in South Carolina. He was the first student minister at the church and had to start from the ground up. We had only a few students, and if one or two were absent, we played basketball in the gym, thinking we didn't have enough students to do anything productive. We were young in age and ministry and for the most part didn't have a clue about what we were doing. We look back on those days and wonder how in the world we made it through those years! Sam often says today that those were some of the best days of our ministry, and if we had known then what we know now, we would have taken advantage of every moment we had with those few students. As we began to build relationships and minister to the students in that church, they began to bring their friends and before we knew it, our numbers had grown to more than twenty teens.

Since that time, we have ministered to students in churches of various sizes. Through all of those situations, we have learned one important thing: regardless of the size of your girls' ministry, small groups are best. If you are involved in a larger church, you still have to divide into small groups for more effective ministry. Larger churches often divide middle school students and high school students. If you are in a smaller church, you have the advantage of having everyone together!

Every church, regardless of size, has its share of advantages and challenges. Guard against looking at other churches and seeing the building and facilities and wishing your church could be like another. Large buildings and modern facilities do not ensure a good church. God's power working through people who follow His leadership makes a good church. Smaller churches may not be able to afford to pay a girls' minister, but they can organize ministry with volunteers to make sure ministry to teen girls happens effectively. If you are in a smaller church, you may find the following tips helpful:

✿ **Start small and grow the ministry only as fast as you can recruit leadership.** If not, you will become overwhelmed by the tasks at hand and girls will not receive the personal attention they need at this critical stage of life.

✿ **Gather resources from various places.** Always keep your eyes open for bargains and items that would be good decorations or gifts for teenage girls. You will often find journals, craft supplies, invitations, or other small gift items on sale that will be useful in girls' ministry events. Purchase and save them until you need them. Also talk to people in your area about your vision for girls' ministry. Often business people or store owners will donate items to help when ministry to teens is involved.

Resist the temptation to view larger numbers as an indication that God is blessing your ministry or that you're doing everything right. Sometimes the greatest ministry takes place within the smallest group.

✿ **Invest in the lives of girls you already have in your church regardless of numbers.** As ministry takes place, the numbers will begin to increase and your ministry will grow. However, never use numbers as the measure or barometer of your success. Resist the temptation to view larger numbers as an indication that God is blessing your ministry or that you're doing everything right. Sometimes the greatest ministry takes place within the smallest group. Pour into the sheep God has called you to shepherd. Let Him worry about how many sheep there are.

✿ **Partner with other churches in your area to pool resources and do events.** Get to know the women who have a heart for girls' ministry in your community. Meet together and share ideas and resources. Talk about the common struggles you face. Pray together. View them as fellow comrades-in-arms in this battle for the hearts and lives of the teen girls you are trying to reach. Never view these other women or their ministries as competition.

And never ever compare others' ministries to yours. Remember, God has placed you in a unique situation. Remain faithful to His calling, not someone else's.

✿ **Plan with excellence and put as much effort into girls' ministry events for four girls as you would for forty girls.** Excellence demonstrates that you care about the ministry. It demonstrates to girls, their parents, and other leaders that ministry to girls is important, not just something you do on the side in your spare time.

✿ **Keep in mind that this generation of girls craves relationships, not excessive programming.** They are disconnected from others and need a place where they can make those connections and learn how to live in relationship with others.

✿ **Look for events that larger churches sponsor and attend with the girls in your church.** Most churches (if not all!) would be more than willing to partner with other churches for ministry to girls. This approach also teaches the girls that we're all a part of one Kingdom and aren't divided because of church size.

Never ever compare others' ministries to yours. Remember, God has placed you in a unique situation. Remain faithful to His calling, not someone else's.

✿ **Use homes to host events for teenage girls.** Homes make events more welcoming and friendly and will allow the girls to see the girls' ministry leaders in their homes in a more relaxed atmosphere.

✿ **Don't give up or become discouraged.** Remember God has a plan for your ministry and your church. Ask God to give you His unique vision for your girls' ministry and start there.

GIRL TALK: THE POWER OF YOUR WORDS
by Pam Gibbs

Gossip. Lying. Language. "Sexting" over cell phones. Trash talk. This Bible study tackles these tough topics with teen girls. This five-session Disciple-Now model Bible study helps girls recognize the power of their words and challenges girls to use their speech to heal rather than hurt. The student book and leader's guide are sold separately.

Leader • 005190069 • $9.95
Learner • 005189797 • $7.95

CONFIDENT
by Carol Sallee

The world tries to fool you into believing you can find the confidence you need in a myriad of ways. Social status. Popularity. Having the right clothes, the right hairstyle, and the right boyfriend. The problem with all of these things is that they are temporary. A girl can go from the "It Girl" to a social outcast in a matter of minutes. Clothing and hairstyles change overnight. Boyfriends come and go. If you build your confidence on these fleeting things, you're going to get stuck. If you're struggling to really live your life to the fullest, then you've come to the right study. It's designed to help you find the confidence that only God can give. The kind of confidence that lasts a lifetime. The kind of confidence that inspires you to take risks. The kind of confidence that looks good on you. Leaders helps included.

005189794 • $10.95

INSIDER: WHAT GUYS ARE THINKING AND WHY YOU NEED TO KNOW
by Shaunti Feldhahn and Lisa Rice

Give teenage girls the thing they've always wanted—the keys to understanding boys. These popular women's authors got their answers straight from the horse's mouth—teen guys. The seven-week, magazine-format resource is packed with articles, quizzes, and devotions designed to shed light on guys and help girls understand their role as fellow believers.

Student Book • 005113491 • $11.95
Leader Guide • 005116687 • $9.95
DVD Kit • 005116688 • $62.95

WOVEN: A RETREAT FOR GIRLS

Contains everything you need to carry out a retreat with a group of teen girls. Includes 10 student books, a leader's guide, promotional posters, and a CD-ROM with extra features such as logos for printing T-shirts or other special gifts, Web links, PowerPoint® presentations, and bonus ideas for small churches, large budgets, and everything in between. Focusing on unity, this retreat will help you address the importance of harmony within your group and among believers of all ages.

Kit • 005190071 • $99.95
Student Book • 005190073 • $6.95
Leader Guide • 005190072 • $8.95

inside *girls ministry*

BLOG
ARTICLES
PRODUCTS
EVENTS
CONTACT

LifeWay | Students

inside girls ministry is a place for you as a leader of teen and preteen girls. Here you will find encouragement, cultural updates, news, and other information that will help you minister to teen girls. Once in a while, we'll update you about girls' resources we are working on and other offerings (training, events,etc.) we provide.

CATEGORIES

LOVE
SEX
BIBLE STUDY
SCHOOL
FRIENDS

SUBSCRIBE

email address

5 Tips for Starting a Girls Ministry at Your Church

posted January 1, 2009 by Pam Gibbs

1. Choose a coordinator for the girls' ministry who has a heart for teenage girls. Titus 2:3-5 gives the qualifications of a woman who is worthy to teach younger women. Prayerful consideration and a sense of God's direction will be imperative as you enlist the person for this important position.

2. Form a team of godly women and diverse girls to study the needs of the teenage girls in your community and church. While the basic needs of girls are similar most everywhere; there will be specific areas of need based on the region in which you live, the family situations in your church, and the culture of your area. This team will work with the girls' ministry coordinator under your supervision.

3. Set up a mission statement and goals in line with the overall mission of the church and youth ministry, but focus on the specific needs of preteen and teenage girls.

4. Recruit, develop, and train leaders. Continually cast the vision for girls' ministry to the girls' ministry team and leadership. Provide resource materials. Pray leaders into their positions as you recruit the ones God is calling to serve.

5. Evaluate the current programs, ministries, and events going on in your youth ministry. Are they meeting the needs of teenage girls? Do they simply need to be tweaked, or do you need to begin something entirely new?

Beginning with these basics – which should all be covered in prayer – will pave the way for God to do some amazing things. For more concrete ideas to begin your

Girls' Ministry Blog

Log on at www.lifeway.com/girlsministry